To deer Kii

Love

Sara Satari

Follow My Footsteps

Martha Ford 3-2018

Follow My Footsteps

୫

A Journey of Adventure, Disaster, and Redemption
Inspired by the Plight of At-Risk Girls

Sara Safari and Jeffrey Kottler

ISBN-13: 9780692725801
ISBN-10: 0692725806

Dedication

This book is dedicated to the courageous and resilient scholarship girls supported by the Empower Nepali Girls Foundation.

We also dedicate this book to our partners and spouses, Matt and Ellen, who have indulged and supported our adventures.

Table of Contents

Preface

THIS IS NOT just a book about mountaineering, about tragedy on the highest mountain on Earth. It is not only a story about the devastating earthquakes that occurred in Nepal in 2015, leaving tens of thousands of people dead and millions without basic shelter, sanitation, food, and water. This is the story of one woman's courage and persistence to bring attention to the plight of Nepali girls who, without support and help, might very well end up forced into early marriage or sex slavery.

This is a tale not only of adventure and of bravery, but also one that highlights how the altruistic efforts of a few can make such a difference in the lives of so many others who have been abandoned, neglected, or abused. It is about how we can inspire and lead others, not just by throwing money at a cause, or telling people what to do and how to do it, but rather through our own daily actions. If we have been successful in assisting and saving hundreds of girls, it has been as much through our relationships with them, our mentoring and connections to them, as any scholarships and financial support that were provided. We have invited them to follow our footsteps.

The structure of the book is somewhat unusual in that the focus of our story is about Sara's experiences and adventures, yet there are several chapters in which we alternate narrators, describing events as they unfolded at the same time in different parts of the world, including Kathmandu, Mount Everest, and the epicenter of the second major earthquake that took place in the Khumbu region near Everest Base Camp.

Although all the events and experiences described in this book occurred as described, the names of some of the individuals mentioned in the story have been changed.

Acknowledgements

NONE OF OUR work, or our adventures, could have been possible without the love and constant support of our spouses, Matt and Ellen, who have been far more than cheerleaders, but also active partners in our mission. We are also grateful to our many friends and family members who have tolerated our long absences while working abroad or climbing mountains in faraway places.

We are most appreciative to Sherry Hester for her help transcribing interviews and editing the manuscript.

We are most grateful to Pasang Temba Sherpa, Babita Gurung, A.D. Sherpa, John Child, Funuru Sherpa, Kumar Bhattarai, Chhusang Sherpa, and the dozens of Nepali volunteers who assist us with our collective work creating opportunities for girls and young women who would not otherwise have a chance for an education.

Sara Safari
Jeffrey Kottler

CHAPTER 1

Sara: The Icefall

April, 2015

"LAZY STEPS," I kept saying to myself over and over again. "Lazy steps." Take it slow and easy, I kept reminding myself. Not so easy when my legs felt like rubber and my pounding heart felt like it was going to implode.

Azim, a climber who had scaled the 13 highest peaks in the world without oxygen, had been watching me the other day and told me I was walking too fast. "Why are you in such a hurry?" he asked me. "Save your energy. You'll need it later."

I was hanging onto a ladder, the fifth one stacked on top of each other against a vertical wall in the Khumbu Icefall, the head of the Mt. Everest glacier that crawls up to four feet each day. This is the part of the journey to the top of Everest that is the most treacherous and unpredictable. It is where the 16 Sherpa guides died in a tragic accident the previous year and where many of the climbers who attempt the summit end up losing their lives. Huge crevasses open and close without warning. Ice towers suddenly collapse, sending blocks of ice the size of cars tumbling down. The glacier is a living, unforgiving being, growing, changing the landscape, and it is difficult to anticipate its next moves.

On April 25, 2015, I had finally negotiated the last stage of the circuitous route, crawling over, up, and around deep crevasses to scale this last wall before arriving at Camp 1 at 20,000 feet with my summit team. Although it was approaching midday, it was snowing and bitterly cold. My legs were tired, but I was still feeling strong as I approached the top of the last ladder. Lazy steps. I was concentrating on timing my exhale to the moment my boot touched the next rung of the ladder. Probably just an hour or two to go.

I stopped for a moment to look around and remind myself where I was and how I had gotten there. It was a wonderland of ice, as if a mad sculptor went wild creating deep, yawning caves, towers and blocks of frozen walls, and fractures that were so deep they didn't seem to have a bottom. I had been training and rehearsing for this part of the climb for two years, arranging ladders on chairs across a room, stepping on each rung with the spiked crampons tied securely on my heavy mountain boots. The truth was that I was terrified every moment we were stuck in this killing zone and I was counting the minutes until we would reach safety.

We had been spending the previous month completing various acclimatizing climbs, going up thousands of feet, then back down to rest and recover, allowing our bodies to adjust. We were heading up to the "death zone," an altitude where jets fly and the human body immediately begins to fall apart. Climbers' lungs fill with liquid. Even with supplemental oxygen the brain stops functioning other than to scream, "Get me out of here!" There are more than 200 bodies buried on the mountain, frozen into ice sculptures. Those lost in the Icefall have now been sucked into the glacier where, in a few hundred years, their bodies make their way back to Base Camp.

Our goal during this trip was to make it up to Camp 2 and back down, then do another training and acclimatizing exercise before heading up to the summit in another few weeks. Things had been going incredibly well. So far, no problems at all. Just dealing with the cold. And the ladders. And the whims of the Icefall.

Inside a Blender

I'd crossed so many ladders I'd lost count, certainly over 50 of them, each one either leaning over a crevasse or propped up against a wall. I much preferred the vertical ones because if I fell, there was at least a chance I could survive as I was solidly anchored. But I was told that if I slipped on one of those high-wire walks across a big canyon, I'd fall all the way back to America. I just kept reminding myself to not look down and take lazy, relaxed, deliberate steps. I heard the scrape of my crampons on the aluminum rungs and concentrated on carefully placing each foot; if I slipped I would likely take out the climbers right behind me.

Our team left Base Camp about 5 AM which was a late start; most of the other teams departed several hours before us to avoid the dangers of melting ice and avalanches once the sun warmed the glacier. There were six climbers and two guides as part of our team and I was right in the middle, right where I preferred to be.

"Clear," I yelled out in a hoarse voice I hardly recognized, just as I got to the top of a ladder. That was my signal that it was safe for those behind me to follow as I started up the next ladder to reach the ledge where we would rest.

The route through the Icefall had been completely changed this year as a result of the tragic deaths that occurred last year when so many people died during an avalanche. The Sherpas had been setting ropes and preparing the route when they perished, once again guaranteeing that nobody would summit that year. We were now following the new pathway that wound through and around the various obstacles standing in our way. And things were going very well indeed: our team was strong—no weak links and each member able to support the others. The weather forecast was excellent. And even with our late start we were making good progress toward Camp 1 and would certainly arrive in just a few more hours.

I could feel almost constant movement and shifting on the ladders, even when they were bolted firmly into the ice. Sometimes they slipped a little from the weight of one or more of us climbing upward or across. The ice itself was always moving, making groaning sounds that almost sounded human.

One of the hundreds of vertical ladders up glacial walls and horizontal ladders stretched across gaping crevasses on the Khumbu Icefall, the most dangerous part of the Everest climb.

I resettled my ice axe into a more comfortable position, and reached up for the next rung of the ladder. I grabbed hold and was preparing to lift up when I could feel that something was terribly wrong. I was certain the ladder was still attached to the wall, yet I could feel everything shifting and shaking to the left, then to the right. I could feel myself falling and yet holding tighter didn't seem to be helping much at all; it was as if the whole mountain was falling. And it was.

All of a sudden it felt like I was inside a blender with whirling snow everywhere and a strong wind that was threatening to blow me off the wall. My brain couldn't process what was happening and I wondered why everything was suddenly exploding all around me. All I could think of to do was grab onto the rope above the ladders and try to pull myself to safety. I could hear someone below screaming, "Avalanche!" but as a girl from Southern California, my brain recognized immediately that this was an earthquake. It would be measured at 7.8 and would kill over 10,000 people, including almost 20 climbers and support staff still at the Base Camp.

No more lazy steps. I was climbing just as fast as I could up that last ladder, pulling on the rope above me, hoping to get to the top before the wall collapsed completely. I looked over my shoulder and saw ice towers falling everywhere. The place where we had stopped for a break just a few minutes earlier was now gone. Completely vanished. If we had rested just another few minutes there, we'd all have been swallowed up by the blinding hurricane of snow.

Big chunks of ice were breaking off to my left and right. I lost all visibility and could now feel the brunt of the avalanche itself burying everything in its path. There was debris and blowing snow everywhere, making it difficult to orient myself. All I cared about was going up, up, up, until finally, I pulled myself over the edge of the wall on my chest. I was hyperventilating, breathing so hard I thought I was going to pass out. I couldn't get enough oxygen into my lungs and every time I did try to draw a breath, it felt like I was drowning. I clipped myself into as many of the anchors and carabineers as I could find, realizing that would do little good if the whole wall collapsed. The wind was blowing so hard I thought I'd take flight, so all I could think to do was hug the ground that was bucking like a bronco.

I wrapped a rope around my hand and arm and tied it off to an anchor, thinking that if and when the wall fell down into the crevasse below I might be able to save myself and climb back out. I was so cold that I could barely grip the rope. My nose and mouth were smothered, as if a cold towel was held over my face. My heart was pounding so hard I thought that I might be having a heart attack. I had to keep reminding myself to hang on and breathe.

I knew the avalanche was just about on top of me as I could feel the whipping wind becoming even stronger. I held onto the rope as tightly as I could and started kicking the spikes of my crampons into the ice to help further stabilize me. There was a moment of complete silence, when everything seemed to pause for a moment—or at least it seemed that way—and I realized I was about to perish. And there was nothing I could do about that except hold on. I kept thinking, this is how people die here. I realized that even with all my training, nothing could have really prepared me for this. I had time to think about the sadness my family would feel, what my husband would do, and my last thought was wondering if they would ever find my body. Strangely, I felt at peace and now accepted that this was how my life would end. I just held on as tightly as I could and waited for whatever would come next.

Through the screaming wind and sounds of crashing ice, I could hear one of the guides yelling up to me, asking if I was okay. I could hear others screaming their locations. But I couldn't move. I was shaking so badly that I couldn't control myself. My legs wouldn't work. All I could do was clench and unclench my hands as they held onto the rope. I tried to take a deep breath and I started sobbing. During the next few hours, our team miraculously found one another, with everyone surviving, and I couldn't stop crying. I could hear through the radio that many people still in Base Camp had been crushed by boulders and ice from the avalanche. I learned that those above us were trapped at Camp 2 and couldn't get down.

I noticed a head peek above the edge of the wall and recognized that it was my tent mate, Kate. We had already been through so much together and I thought for sure that the mountain had taken her. Her face was grim but determined as she held up her hand to me and said, "I can't feel my fingers. I'm so cold. I think my fingers are gone." As I started to crawl over to her, I felt the mountain shift once again and I grabbed on tighter to my rope.

I started to freak out even more after recognizing my friend, thinking that this mother of four might lose all her fingers. Somehow that struck me as even more terrible than us merely being buried alive. I started to hyperventilate again and couldn't catch my breath. I flipped over on my back and saw nothing but the swirling snow above me. We were trapped up here and there was no way down. The ladders were gone.

All is Lost

Once our team had regrouped at the top of the wall, we stood holding one another. Reports were now coming in via radios and satellite phones about the extent of the devastation throughout Nepal, over 100,000 children left homeless, thousands buried under rubble in Kathmandu, and whole villages wiped out in the Annapurna Himalayan range further west of us. I had assumed by now that friends and family back home had heard the news and must assume I was gone, swallowed by the Icefall. The mountain had once again shut down all attempts to climb her and it would be a second year with nobody making it to the summit.

Although all I wanted to do was sit down in the snow and rest, compose myself, the guides kept urging us further upward to safety. There was no trail anymore; everything had been wiped out by the avalanche. There were more ladders to climb but now they were wobbly, unstable, barely anchored to the ice. We worried about the people below us, and above us: how could they have possibly survived? Yet, we kept moving.

Once we arrived to Camp 1, the first thing I noticed was one of the guides from another team was standing in front of a tent crying. He had just heard the news about all the people who had died at Base Camp, but all I could think about were the girls that we support in this region.

I had vowed to reach the summit in order to plant the flag of the charity I support: Empower Nepali Girls. For the past several years we had been identifying mostly lower caste girls who were at highest risk to be trafficked into sex slavery, or forced into early marriage, and we raised funds to mentor and provide scholarships to keep them in school and out of harm's way. There were over 300 girls in our program, most of them the first in their villages to ever attend higher education. Our first girls were now studying to become doctors, nurses, teachers, and engineers. They had never before met women with professional careers or women who had attempted such male-dominated sports as mountaineering. The girls looked up to me—as a professor, an engineer, a woman of color like them, who had overcome such challenges in the male-dominated world of the Middle East. They were amazed that I was stronger than most men, could climb higher and further than anyone else they knew. It inspired them. It gave them faith. It showed them what might be possible for their own lives. But now all those dreams may very well have been crushed by the earthquake. So many of them would have lost their homes, their schools, and all their hope.

I had vowed to raise $1 for each foot of Everest (29,028 feet) to help the girls, and was successful in more than doubling that goal. But now it seemed that everything was lost, all my dreams for the children, even for my own life. I could do nothing but cry no matter how much others tried to comfort me. I had worked so hard, for so long, to bring attention to the plight of our children in Nepal, many of whom would now likely disappear and give up their education.

A Dangerous Rescue

The camp doctor, Julie, took one look at me and realized how much trouble I was in. My brain was scrambled and so traumatized I lost track of where I was and what I was doing there. I was lost and disoriented, shivering as much from terror as the penetrating cold that was settling in. Julie forcibly picked me up off the ground, yelling through the gale-force winds, "Sara. Sara! You have to get inside or you are going to die!" She dragged me, pulling me inside a tent and then began to undress me, untying my boots and crampons, no easy task considering that the laces and straps were frozen solid. I was shivering, shaking, still sobbing, when the last thing I remember before passing out was the sound of Julie's voice telling me everything would be okay.

I awoke from my stupor an indeterminate amount of time later to the sound of voices outside, frantic voices sharing scraps of information about all the people who were dead, the villages destroyed. Once I managed to reassemble myself, physically and mentally, change into dry, warm clothes, I stepped outside and learned that we were all now trapped on the mountain with limited supplies and food to sustain us. There was no longer any way back through the Icefall, and some people were saying that they didn't think a helicopter rescue up here at this altitude and in these conditions was even possible. Even if we could somehow make it back to Base Camp, there was no longer any trail for the weeklong walk back to the airport in Lukla from where we would be able to journey home.

I crawled back into the tent and passed out once again, awakened several hours later by another earthquake and the roar of an avalanche barreling down on Nuptse, the mountain right next to us. I could hear one of our guides yelling to close our tents and keep our helmets on at all times in case the tents broke loose from their moorings.

For two nights I stayed trapped in the tent, hoping for rescue. Most of the time I was so exhausted and cold, all I could do was just stay huddled in my sleeping bag with all my clothes on. I still couldn't stop crying. Aftershocks were now coming every few hours, terrifying us further that we wouldn't last until a helicopter could (hopefully) make it up to retrieve us. I kept thinking about my husband, Matt, my mother and my family, and how much they would be worried about me and wondering if I was still okay. But most of all I worried about all our girls down below and how they were managing if they had lost their homes, if they had even survived.

*Everest Base Camp after the avalanche that killed 20
climbers and injured more than 150 others.*

Finally, after so many agonizing hours of uncertainty, fear, cold, discomfort, and increasingly horrific news about the extent of the damage and death toll, I was awakened (although I never really slept much) by the muffled sound of a helicopter landing near our camp. The air was so thin, and the winds so treacherous, the pilot started throwing stuff out the door to lighten the load—chairs, extraneous equipment, anything not bolted on. We were told to leave everything and that only the lightest and smallest among us could escape first. It was the one time I can remember feeling so grateful for my small size.

We landed at Base Camp a few minutes later where we were unloaded so that the pilot could try to rescue those who had been left behind. Just a few days earlier, this place had been as happy as revelers at Disneyland with everyone so excited about their upcoming summit attempts. It had been party city with music blaring, people staying up most of the night talking and drinking and telling stories about their prior adventures, comparing notes about their world travels. Now it was a ghost town, except the ghosts were still very much present. I could see blood-spattered clothes on the ground, huge boulders that had crushed tents with everyone inside. Brightly colored gear was scattered all across the mountain and the survivors were wandering around searching for their friends' bodies.

It took five more days living in this graveyard before another helicopter could retrieve us and fly us back to the airport in Lukla. I had been greatly looking forward to actually walking back so I could visit with our girls once again who lived along the trail and tell them about my adventures, share tea and boiled potatoes with their families, and also help them with their schoolwork. I had been collecting as much extra food and snacks as I could from the other climbers so I could distribute them to the families, knowing that they would have lost everything. As soon as the helicopter landed, I rushed out the door and started making my way to some of our children's homes in Lukla, or what was left of them. One of our girls, Manila, recognized me right away and escorted me around the village so I could check on the children and distribute food where it was most needed.

"Please don't forget us," the girls would say over and over to me, a frequent refrain we hear so often because many trekkers and climbers who come to Nepal make promises they never keep. Our organization has been doing this work for over 15 years so we had earned some degree of trust in the area, but the children always feared we would forget and neglect them as so many had before. I promised them, over and over, I would be back, that I would never, ever forget them. I told them I would help them to rebuild their homes and schools—and their lives.

Once landing back in Kathmandu, the capital city, I learned that the devastation in the Everest area was only one region that had been affected by the earthquake. The capital city, thousands of years old and

Two of our scholarship girls I visited before flying back to Kathmandu. They had lost their home, and all their possessions, after the earthquake.

filled with ancient monasteries and temples, was now wrecked beyond belief. The tectonic plates underneath had literally and permanently lifted the city several feet and shifted it 10 feet further south, knocking down so many of the ancient structures made of brick and mud. So many of our scholarship girls, who had been working so hard to create opportunities for themselves, were now left with nothing.

CHAPTER 2

— ❧ —

Jeffrey: Ring Around the Rosie

May, 2015

"Ring around the rosie, a pocketful of posies, ashes, ashes, we all fall DOWN!"

I was holding hands with four young children between the ages of 3 and 7, as we circled round and round before falling in a heap on the ground in giggles. It was two weeks since the first major earthquake and while Sara had finally made it back to the capital city and was organizing relief efforts with our volunteers, I had just arrived in Nepal.

There had been little sleep for me during this interval because of the 12-hour time change which meant that I was receiving messages from children in the middle of the night.

"My house is gone," one 12-year-old girl wrote me. "I can't find my parents. I don't know what to do. Please help me!" Others were saying that they had no food or water and asked where they should go to find help.

I was fielding calls about Sara as well, people wondering whether she had survived the disaster. I was trying to organize medical teams and bring supplies into the country. I had heard that Nepali officials were turning back volunteers and were not allowing medical or relief supplies into the country without paying hefty duty (bribes). There were millions of dollars of foreign aid and supplies sitting on the tarmac at the airport that had not yet been allowed to enter through customs. Meanwhile many people had no food, no uncontaminated water, no shelter, or even blankets to cover themselves. There were no working sanitation or toilet facilities in many areas, increasing the risk of spreading cholera, encephalitis, and other diseases because of all the bodies buried beneath the collapsed buildings.

Just as Sara headed back home to recover, we missed one another as I arrived in Kathmandu with a medical team and bags full of equipment, supplies, surgical tools, and other resources. We had just arrived from the airport to our headquarters where there were one hundred of our children waiting with their families. Our volunteers had erected a big tent, set away from any of the buildings nearby that could pose a danger during one of the many aftershocks. We were serving food and water, as well as playing games with the children.

Four children held onto my hands as we circled round and round, singing "Ring around the rosie." We chanted over and over, pulling one another in a ragged, giggly circle. That this nursery rhyme is sometimes attributed to a description of the "rosy rash" of the Great Plague in Europe, as well as the cremation of bodies, escaped us at the time. But as we rested, looking around at the hundreds of others gathered together for a free medical clinic we had organized, I felt the ground start to vibrate, then buckle underneath, throwing us to the ground. I heard children screaming and crying, distracted by the realization that I was no longer standing but sitting in the grass. I looked up to see buildings swaying violently, cracks in the walls appearing like spidery webs, bricks falling, structures crumbling. Everyone was running away from the buildings in terror, fearful that they would be crushed like the thousands of others who had died in the quake that occurred two weeks prior. I was holding onto the children, trying to soothe them, but my brain couldn't yet quite fathom that this was a major earthquake, 7.3 on the Richter Scale. The epicenter was about 50 miles away near the Tibetan Border, a locale that I would soon visit with our medical/trauma team to provide the only assistance they would see in the foreseeable future.

Five minutes after this photo was taken, a second major 7.3 earthquake knocked us to the ground, as well as many of the buildings that remained standing precariously after the first quake a few weeks earlier. The aftershocks would continue for months afterwards, forcing everyone to live outside.

I Can Still Hear the Children Screaming

Sara had returned home to spread word of the disaster in Nepal that was already being relegated to old news. We needed to raise hundreds of thousands of dollars during the next few weeks in order to help families resettle themselves in temporary housing. The monsoon rains were about to begin and hundreds of thousands of people were now homeless and without any resources. We needed to distribute clean water, rice, sanitation supplies, tents, blankets, clothing, plus medical supplies and services to those who had been injured. Given that the government was being so uncooperative, and the southern neighbor of India was about to close the border in protest to the new constitution that would soon be finally ratified, the shortages of food, medicine, and fuel were about to become a lot worse. There would be lines miles long of buses and cars waiting for three or more days in order to obtain a few gallons of petrol on the black market.

Nepal is a landlocked nation without any natural resources, trapped between the two superpowers of India and China. The government in Nepal at the time was at a standstill. The devastation by the earthquake followed ten years of civil war, Maoists funded by China to protest the corrupt monarchy and the assassination of the last king. Thus far, very little aid or medical help was getting into the country, or at least past the airport. Sara was home doing her best to raise money to support the earthquake relief effort in addition to fund our scholarship girls in 14 villages around the country.

Along with several nurses, an ex-special forces medic, and some medical assistants, we had set up a clinic to treat people with a variety of health problems from respiratory infections to wounds, as well as soothe the fears of our scholarship girls who had nowhere else to go. Many of the children were having nightmares and sometimes during the day they would break out sobbing uncontrollably. Schools were no longer in session, mostly because the buildings were no longer safe. Aftershocks continued almost every few hours, making it unwise to enter any building. Even today, I still have involuntary startle responses every time I hear a loud noise or feel something moving. I never go into a room without checking carefully for the nearest exit.

The Nepali government was asking all foreign aid workers to leave the country. Thus far I hadn't seen many relief or aid workers anywhere, except a few representatives of the Red Cross from Europe and Japan who were now preparing to exit since they were not welcome. Pretending our team members were trekkers and our dozens of duffel bags were filled with climbing equipment instead of surgical supplies, antibiotics, and other medications, we kept a low profile when taking off in a small plane to arrive at what has been described as the most dangerous airport in the world, Lukla, the gateway to Everest. The runway is built on a steep upward angle that abruptly ends at the base of a mountain. Pilots are required to thread through high peaks, make a sharp left turn, and then (hopefully) land and hit the brakes before running out of room. The takeoff is even more terrifying since sometimes the plane actually drops off the end of the runway on its downward slant before gaining altitude for the trip home.

We landed safely in Lukla but the place seemed mostly abandoned. After exiting the plane, we put on our packs and began walking on what used to be the Everest Base Camp Trail but was now reduced to washed out, broken hillsides. Avalanches had virtually wiped out most of the usual route, requiring us to walk along precarious cliff faces where there once stood teahouses and homes but now were covered in rubble. The mud that had been used as mortar between the stone huts had virtually liquefied, crumbling the structures to piles of rocks. In many cases, they formed the graves of family members who had been trapped inside.

As we walked along our improvised route, we distributed tents and sanitation supplies to people we found along the way. The schools we had supported all these years were now almost completely destroyed, but we used a few of their intact rooms to set up our medical clinics. All it took was for us to hang out a sign reading "Free Medical Clinic" in order for hundreds of people to come streaming in from the hillsides. Most of them had never seen a doctor or nurse before, never had their blood pressure or respiration checked, so they were fascinated by this opportunity not only to have their wounds dressed and their infections treated, but also to have a real medical professional check them out. Matt, our medic, had operated previously during combat in the Middle East, so he was well prepared to deal with some of the chaos and "battlefield" conditions we encountered along the way.

Most of the children were shell-shocked and tearful, not at all surprising considering that almost everything they'd ever known and every meager possession were now gone. Many of them had lost relatives. One of our scholarship girls told us that her grandfather was so disturbed and freaked out by the earth constantly moving and shaking that he threw himself in the river to take his own life. It turns out this wasn't that unusual considering that several dozen people each day were committing suicide, having given up all hope. Hundreds of others just keeled over from heart attacks, their brains and hearts unable to handle the constant stress and uncertainty.

We have over 100 scholarship girls we support in the Everest region and they were easy to recognize because they were wearing our trademark Empower Nepali Girls down jackets in bright, primary colors. The girls I met along the way kept asking about Sara, whether she was okay, whether she will return soon to see them. Sara is their heroine, the woman they someday wish to become—poised, self-assured, accomplished, strong, and not dependent on anyone. They have lived in a world all their lives in which their caste, their tribe, their gender and station in life, have set rigid limits about what they are permitted to do. They can't inherit land. Their families can't afford to send them to school, since boys are first given that opportunity. They are denied entry into the best schools, largely because their own education and resources are limited. But Sara gives them hope that they can change their circumstance and become engineers, teachers, mountaineers, anything they want.

Trauma, Trauma Everywhere

Before we departed for the Everest region that Sara just left, the epicenter of the last earthquake, we scrambled to get our supplies together. Riots had broken out protesting the government inaction, and people were trying to escape the capital. Politicians were afraid to show their faces for fear they would be killed by everyone who was so furious at the chaos and incompetence of the government. Our plan was to provide basic healthcare, distribute antibiotics to those with respiratory infections, and distribute medical supplies to clinics in the areas. I also prepared simple treatment manuals for responding to the most acute psychological trauma symptoms and the more severe cases that will start appearing in a few months when we return with another team.

I used to think seeing ten patients a day in psychotherapy was pretty challenging, but we treated 158 medical and 41 counseling cases at the medical/trauma clinic we set up in two school classrooms. This was the first of five that we planned for the hardest hit areas. People from all around the area lined up patiently outside our "offices." While Matt, our medic, Monet, our triage specialist, and two of our Nepali scholarship girls who were now nurses, worked furiously to treat broken bones, abrasions, infections, wounds, and all kinds of trauma-related symptoms, I worked with various families, children, adults, and couples. At one point there were so many people lined up at the door toward the end of the day I just invited them all in for a group session.

Our trauma treatment center in one village operated out of a school that still had a few classrooms intact. Chhusang Sherpa, a high school student, functioned as a translator and assistant.

With Chhusang Sherpa, age 17, acting as my interpreter and assistant, I talked to people about their nightmares, insomnia, hypervigilance, and struggles losing their homes. The few in the region who were willing to talk about their fears felt isolated and alone, as if they were the ones who were weak; one woman told me her husband and children accused her of being "cowardly" because she startled so easily and refused to enter their house, preferring to sleep outside.

I visited with two 70-year-old friends together presenting various chronic medical complaints for which our medic and nurses had no treatments. They were both extremely hard of hearing so I kept yelling (through Chhusang) that their symptoms became worse because of the stress they were under. I saw a family concerned about their 5-year-old son who had been trapped in a building during the first earthquake and was now mute. Next, I spoke with two young mothers and their children who wanted to talk about their fears because they said nobody else would listen. They reported that most of their neighbors and family were acting as if things were normal, making it difficult to tell their stories.

I barely had time for a break to empty my bladder before I noticed the line outside my room getting longer, and the prospective patients were becoming anxious and restless. The tremors continued, making all of us nervous. I constantly rehearsed in my head the safest route outside every time I felt the ground shake. Before I could even get resettled in my chair, an older woman stuck her head in the door expectantly. I invited her in and learned that she really wanted to see our doc, but because he was busy, she came to see me instead. She reached out her hands to hold my own and just looked into my eyes for the longest time. I wasn't exactly sure what we were doing but I just followed her lead. Then, abruptly, she thanked me, smiled, and walked out the door, holding it open for an even older fellow who shuffled in. He told me he was 96 years old, in remarkably good health for his age, but thought his time had come and he was going to die soon. He just wanted me to know a bit about his life before it ended. He must have enjoyed our conversation because later I saw him standing in line again for another session.

There were cases where I was so far outside of my usual standards of care that I could only shake my head in wonderment. One man complained of vertigo, which made perfect sense to me since I had also been dizzy since the earthquakes, feeling as if the ground was constantly moving (which it was!). I reassured him the symptoms would go away but he insisted on some medication to make him feel better. So I "prescribed" some little orange pills, one in the morning before breakfast and one in the evening before dinner and he'd feel better. They were aspirin.

I saw a 6-year-old boy and his family because of their concern that he wasn't "normal" since the earthquake. I tried to engage the fellow but he just kept hugging his mother. I welcomed a mother who broke her arm saving her child from a collapsed building during yesterday's earthquake and she had refused to go to the hospital to get it X-rayed and fixed. Matt sent her to me to persuade her to go or she might lose the function of her arm. I tried to be gentle but during the translation Chhusang scolded her and told her she owed it to her child to take care of herself. I looked at Chhusang with awe and admiration: in the time we'd spent together this high school girl was becoming quite the counselor herself.

Our trauma team consisted of a Special Forces medic, hospital administrator, psychologist, several nurses and medical assistants, plus dozens of volunteer social work students. We treated 800 patients suffering from injuries, wounds, infections, depression, and traumatic stress.

I tried all kinds of things during the sessions, normalizing their fears, explaining about trauma and its symptoms, inviting them to share their stories, teaching deep breathing and relaxation strategies, introducing a little self-talk, encouraging them to talk to others, literally holding them, but I found what often worked best, especially with the children, was sharing with them that I felt much the same way they did, out of control, scared, and overreacting to any sound or movement. We mostly laughed about that together.

I've been working with symptoms of trauma all of my professional career, whether the lingering effects of child abuse, sexual abuse, neglect, violence, or natural disasters. I've written many books on the subject that summarize the research and optimal treatment strategies. I've taught classes and workshops on creative interventions for the symptoms, whether using mindfulness-based strategies, cognitive self-talk, support groups, or relational connections. I had expected I'd have to adapt my treatment approaches to fit the rather unique situation that we now faced. Although I'd been to Nepal more than 20 times in the past 15 years, I was still quite ignorant and misinformed about certain cultural traditions. My knowledge of the language was about the same level as a preschooler. I've done lots of "brief therapy" before but not when I'm limited to 15-minute sessions because there were so many people clamoring for attention. I was able to make adjustments and adaptations for these limitations, at least to a certain extent. But what caught me most off guard was that I was now experiencing many of the same symptoms reported by my patients. I was constantly on edge. I couldn't sleep—and when I did manage to fall unconscious—one of the frequent aftershocks would awaken me with my heart pounding in panic. Most disturbing of all was that I would suddenly, and without warning, just start sobbing. This frightened me most of all because it was like someone, or something inside me, would just burst out in tears. Much of the time I didn't know what I was crying about except for perhaps the accumulative horrors that I'd witnessed and experienced.

For months after I returned home, many of my symptoms continued. I was standing in front of a big lecture class at my university, talking to graduate students about relationship issues in the practice of psychotherapy. While I was speaking I had a flashback, thinking about one of our scholarship girls with whom I am particularly close. I was remembering her telling me that there was no point in continuing her education since everything in her life was now destroyed. It felt like everything I'd worked so hard to create all these years was now gone.

CHAPTER 3

――― ✌ ―――

Sara: Back Home

May, 2015

BEING BACK HOME felt unreal. I kept thinking about one of the last girl's homes that I visited, a tiny one-room dwelling of stone and mud. There didn't even seem to be enough room for one person to sleep there but the girl, her parents, and brother, all managed to somehow share the space. Now, even that was gone.

When I arrived at the airport in Los Angeles my family was there to greet me, showering me with flowers and signs welcoming me back. After hugging me they started checking my fingers to make sure they were all still there. I didn't know what to say to anyone. I looked at my husband and he seemed to have aged with worry. I felt terribly guilty, not only for the concern I'd inflicted on everyone, but also because I was home and not with the girls who needed me so badly.

The first question my family asked me, before we were even settled in the car, was whether I planned to return to Nepal any time soon. I shrugged and just stared out the window but they could read the signs and it made them mad. "That's ridiculous! You can't go back there ever again! That mountain almost killed you."

I didn't know what to say. I just felt numb and empty, like I had left a part of myself on Everest and I didn't know if I'd ever regain what I'd lost. I had planned to leave letters, notes, and little stuffed animals representing our scholarship girls near the summit but all of those things were lost in the avalanche, blown across the Himalayas. While sitting at home I just stared at my duffel bags stuffed with climbing equipment, the things I was able to retrieve. I couldn't bring myself to open the bags because every single item reminded me of what happened and everything I wanted to forget. I just sat there and cried, something I'd been doing a lot of since I returned home.

My aunt called me from Iran to make sure I was safe and healthy. She asked me to promise her I would never return to Nepal. She told me it was time to have babies like a good Persian wife. A woman like me didn't belong in those mountains. "Sara," she scolded me, "soon you will be 40. It is time for you to settle down."

She was referring to her sister, my mother, who already had four kids by the time she was 27 and now I was 34 with no children in sight, unless we counted all my 300 daughters in Nepal. "I'm not ready yet," I tried to explain. "I have some things I need to do first." I wasn't exactly sure what those things might be, but I was trying to renege on an earlier promise that I'd start a family after I finished with Everest and my mountaineering career. I was pretty certain I wouldn't be going back up on that mountain any time soon, but I also wanted—needed—to return to Nepal as soon as possible.

Everyone was worried about me, my husband, Matt, most of all. It was obvious I was not the same person anymore. Something had changed in me and I wasn't clear yet what that was all about. I still felt crippled and traumatized, awaking in the middle of the night in terror. Matt would hold me and comfort me, but I could tell that this had worn him down.

Maybe I needed to go away somewhere to take care of myself. I was remembering that before I attempted one of my training climbs on a Tibetan peak, I had spent 10 days at a silent, meditation retreat to clear my mind. It was one of the hardest things I'd ever done, in its own way just as challenging as climbing a Himalayan summit. I never knew I could sit quietly from 4 AM to 9 PM for 10 straight days with no other distractions. Maybe I needed to do something like that again, I wondered.

When the feelings started flooding back into me, I felt such incredible shame and guilt that I had failed the climb, and the girls, so miserably. I was supposed to empower them by my efforts and all I did was become a burden to the many brave people who rescued me. Meanwhile, I was back in my comfortable world with all the luxuries of electricity, hot water, fresh food, clean water, and I thought constantly of all the children who were living outside with nothing except a blanket. The monsoon floods would be starting any day and I couldn't imagine how people would cope. In a way, I envied Jeffrey who was there helping people while I enjoyed luxuries and my ordinary routines.

"But you *did* empower the girls," one friend reassured me. He could tell I was depressed. "You raised all that money for them, far more than you ever imagined possible. And the only thing that could have stopped you from reaching the summit was the biggest earthquake ever recorded in that part of the world. I'd guess those girls are damn proud of you!"

I knew I was fortunate to have survived when so many others perished, but I just couldn't allow myself to be happy when so many others were suffering. And truthfully, I was embarrassed to see all my friends and trainers at the gym, having to admit that I couldn't make it to the top. Everyone said they were so proud of what I had already accomplished, but nothing seemed to have much impact, that is, until my friends reassured me that they were now totally on board with my mission to help me raise even more money for earthquake relief efforts. I knew that Jeffrey and the rest of our team at Empower Nepali Girls were already raising hundreds of thousands of dollars after PayPal designated us as one of their recommended charities to assist the earthquake relief and recovery efforts.

Slowly I started to feel a glimmer of hope and could feel my energy and motivation starting to return, little by little. On the other hand, I didn't like myself very much these days. I'd lost my self-confidence. I complained constantly. I felt sad and moody. And I felt terribly guilty about leaving my husband alone for so many months during my training and climb. Matt has been extraordinarily supportive of my plans and (almost) never complained about my long absences or neglect of him. In my Persian culture I received a lot of grief from others, telling me that women shouldn't do this sort of thing or that my role was to remain at home and take care of my husband. When I heard these things it made me even *more* determined to show our girls in Nepal that women can do *anything* that men can do. I think one of the reasons the girls follow me is because they know that I come from a place that has so many similar restrictions for what girls are allowed to do. The fact that I'm an engineer, and a professor, and a mountain climber, gives them hope that perhaps they, too, can rise above the limitations placed on them by their caste, gender, and poverty.

I knew I couldn't do any of the things I do without Matt's help and support. He probably got more disparaging questions than I did from others. "Why do you let your wife do this?" someone would say to him, as if I needed his permission and blessing.

"I've actually never been all that bothered by guys saying something to me," Matt admitted with a smile. "And if someone does say something, I tell them that I'd never interfere because it's really not my choice. I love Sara for who she is and changing her would mean changing my love for her as well. And I'm certainly not timid about speaking up when the situation calls for it."

Matt recalled one time when the father of a friend of his made a comment to him. "You shouldn't let your wife be so financially independent. Women are really bad at dealing with money issues."

"Oh yeah?" Matt responded to him. "So, how's *your* marriage?"

The guy was divorced, mostly as a result of his over-controlling nature.

And, of course. I would never take such risks or search for adventures unless Matt was on board with my plans. He actually tried to accompany me on many of my excursions, at least for part of the time when he could get away from work, but he also struggled with severe joint problems that made it difficult for him to climb or hike very far. So we both had to put up with a lot of criticism from others in our culture because others just didn't think it was right that a Persian woman would do the things that I do.

When I think about the women in Iran, Nepal, or elsewhere in the world, who are treated so poorly and are not even allowed a basic education, it just makes me furious and more determined to show them that we can be different, in spite of the attempts to oppress us. I felt responsible for keeping this dream alive, but I also felt such a terrible, overwhelming burden. And there were times when I just wanted to give up, give in, and just do what others expected of me.

I'd been watching the news several times during the day to find out what was happening in Nepal. I knew that Jeffrey was out there somewhere, totally isolated, maybe even stranded, and I wondered how they were all doing. According to all the reports I heard and read, things were becoming increasingly worse, not better. People were living in tent cities without any sanitation facilities. There was no safe drinking water and food was scarce. I'd read how very few temporary shelters were available. And yet I still felt even more guilt. One night I was sitting in a restaurant, perfectly comfortable, enjoying great Italian pasta, and the children half the world away from me had nothing to eat. I just broke out crying and everyone looked at me like I was crazy (which is how I really felt).

"Is there something wrong?" the waitress asked me with real concern. I don't think it's very often that she encountered someone who tasted their gourmet spinach and artichoke ravioli in lobster sauce and then broke out in tears.

I tried to explain to her that I wasn't crying because of the food but because of something else—and when I started to describe what happened, Matt interrupted me and asked if I might like to step outside. I was making a scene in the restaurant that others were finding embarrassing. But I couldn't help it; I was *that* out of control.

Interrogations

Several weeks later I went to visit my mother in Arizona and she had created an incredible birthday cake for me that was shaped exactly like Mt. Everest. She had meticulously built the cake to scale, adding pictures of the various stages of the climb on sugar paper that had been attached to the cake. I could clearly see little photos of me standing outside my tent, pressed into the whipped cream that looked just like snow. There was a flag with Empower Nepali Girls perched on top, just like I had always planned to do when I reached the summit.

Although I was concerned my family wouldn't support my effort to climb Everest on behalf of our scholarship girls, my mother created this birthday cake to honor and encourage me, as well as to show her pride at what I was doing.

I had tears in my eyes, grateful tears, but sad ones as well. I was so appreciative of what my mother had done—and yet it brought back all my feelings of failure. "I want you to look at the cake," my mother said to me gently. "I want you to see that you're bigger than Everest, and that you don't have to climb it again. You already put the flag on top of the mountain." Then, she, too, broke out crying and we hugged one another.

A little later, while we were sitting at the table eating the cake, my sister said to me fairly abruptly, "So, are you planning to go back?"

I hesitated for a moment, knowing there was only one right answer she wanted to hear. "I don't know," I finally said just above a whisper. "I haven't decided yet."

I could see the flash of anger in her eyes. "I just don't understand how you can be so selfish!" she yelled at me. "You put all of us through such torture. We thought you were dead, for crying out loud!" Then both my parents and my sister started crying. I knew that they weren't just upset with me, but there were other family crises going on and I was a nice distraction. My brother had been struggling with a number of personal problems and now his health was in jeopardy.

I just didn't answer and kept my mouth closed. I didn't know what to say to them, or even what I could say other than that I was sorry I had put them through such anguish. They just didn't understand why I was so stubbornly focused on pushing my limits or testing myself. And like so many others within my community, they didn't understand why I was doing all of this for a bunch of girls in some obscure country halfway around the world that they'd barely heard of. "Why aren't you helping Iranian girls?" I would frequently be asked. "Don't you think your first priority should be to help your own people?" But I wondered who *are* my people? I'm very proud of my Persian culture and heritage. I love the Farsi language. Yet as concerned as I was about what had been happening in my native country, I believed strongly that offering support to marginalized girls is a global issue unrestricted by any national borders or loyalty to one nation.

It wasn't until I was pushed by my family to declare I wouldn't return to Nepal, or climb any more mountains, that an idea came together for me. I'm not sure if it happened right there at the dinner table with my family or if it slowly took more concrete form over the following days. I realized that there were some valuable, if unintended, lessons in my story. Maybe what I really needed to teach the girls was that striving for a goal is not about attaining it the first time you try. After all, many of our girls have had so little educational support that there is no possible way they could pass entrance exams to university the first time they tried. It was about resilience and persistence that mattered most. It was about not giving up no matter how difficult things get. I wasn't actually thinking about trying Everest again any time soon, but I was considering how closely I was being watched by the girls to see how I handled my disappointment.

Thereafter, every time someone interrogated or challenged or shamed me for putting myself in jeopardy, or not acting like a proper Persian woman, I just kept silent and nodded my head. My main concern was how Matt was dealing with all of it. I would constantly hear people say to him, "Your wife, Sara, she's so strong. She's a real badass." Matt would just smile and agree, but I could tell it bothered him that the subtext of these comments was really something like, "What the hell's wrong with you that you can't control your wife?" But it just made me love him even more because he is such a good guy, and so secure within himself, that he could just seemingly shrug off these rude statements. But still, I could tell it bothered him.

It was usually the men in my culture who would give us the most grief, apparently threatened by the idea that a woman could do things they could not. "I think it's fine that you raise money for these children," one man said to me, as if I needed his approval to continue my efforts. "But this mountain climbing you do? That's got to stop. Are you committing suicide? What's *wrong* with you? And how can you do this to your husband and your family?"

Like so many others, he was telling me that I was not behaving properly in my role as a wife and a woman. I would hear things like this all the time when I would speak at Persian events that had been organized as fundraisers. I gave a talk at one Middle Eastern cultural center and there were three questions I was asked to respond to: (1) Why wasn't I helping Iranian girls instead of these worthless, lower caste children in Nepal?

(2) Why was I doing this since climbing is for men? (3) Does my husband let me do this sort of thing? Matt was actually standing in the back of the room and he yelled out to the audience that I had his complete support. After that, he got lots of strange looks from the other men in attendance. I think they were hoping their wives or girlfriends didn't get any new ideas.

Redoubling My Efforts

Once I realized that my "climb" wasn't over and I could actually continue the journey working on behalf of our girls in Nepal, I started to plan ways I could help spread awareness of their dangerous situation. How awful is it to consider that girls, some as young as 11 or 12 years old, were forcibly pressed into sex slavery? Or much less dramatic, but nevertheless tragic, requiring young girls to marry some older man, just to get her out of the house because the family couldn't afford to feed her?

Since I was one of the "survivors" of the Everest disaster, media and news outlets were regularly contacting me for interviews. Everyone wanted to hear my story, the woman caught in an avalanche on Everest who was trying to bring greater awareness to the problems of neglected children. This led to increasing numbers of speaking engagements and media appearances. I was a novice at this public speaking, but I did my best to just simply tell my story of what happened, talk about the challenges of our girls, and then ask people to help us by donating money for the cause. Several times I spoke at events across the region, doing slide presentations, and also soliciting donations. These events were packed and the audiences were incredibly responsive and supportive. But it was hard. Maybe not as hard as having to slip out of a tent at 19,000 feet, with 50 MPH gale force winds threatening to blow me off the mountain, just to use the toilet facilities on the side of a glacier, but it presented some different challenges.

After I returned from Nepal, I began speaking at fund-raising events to spread awareness of the plight of our girls after the earthquakes. The media was also quite interested in my story as one of the survivors of the avalanche, and also someone who was climbing Everest for something beyond personal accomplishment and glory.

The first appearances had gone so well that I was singularly unprepared for one at a hiking/climbing store that was a terrible disappointment. Although more than 60 people had said that they would be attending, only a handful actually showed up, and I think they were those who just happened to be shopping in the store at the time. I noticed one such shopper standing in the back of the room with an armful of fleece jackets. Even worse, none of them decided to donate anything, even after my most impassioned pleas and tragic images of the children. I felt it was a colossal waste of time.

I knew there was a theme here that was once again familiar. I attempted a very difficult new challenge (studying engineering, teaching computer science, mountaineering, public speaking). Initially, I enjoyed tremendous success, became cocky and overconfident, self-assured to the point I expected everything to go as planned. Inevitably there was some setback, disappointment, failure, perhaps an earthquake of sorts, and I became inconsolably discouraged. But the story in this book is about courage and resilience, even in the face of impossible odds. I'm not speaking about my own experience, but rather what our girls face every day of their lives when they attempt to break the mold from which they were shaped.

Just like training for the mountains, the more I rehearsed and practiced my new skills as a fundraiser and public speaker, the more I was able to improve. I used to hate asking people for money and now I was learning that it really wasn't so hard at all when I wasn't asking for myself but for others who were so desperate. If people declined to help, it no longer bothered me; I just focused instead on whoever *was* willing to help.

I remember visiting an elementary school to give a talk and one third-grade girl came up to me afterwards and proudly announced that she had recently opened up her own personal savings account.

"That's great," I encouraged her, looking around for the door to make my exit. By now the children had all dispersed back to their classrooms, but this one little 10-year-old girl was still looking up at me, waiting for something.

"Um, so I was saying," she continued, "I have, like, two hundred dollars in my account."

"I see," I answered, not seeing at all where this was going.

"So, I was thinking that because it's my own account and it's new and all. I told you I just opened it?"

"Uh huh."

"Well, then I should probably leave at least a little money in the account. But I was wondering? I mean, would it be okay if I donated a hundred and fifty dollars to the girls?"

I was absolutely floored. My mouth fell open and I just didn't know what to say.

"So, would that be okay?" she asked me again.

I just nodded my head.

"And when I grow up," she said looking me right in the eyes, "I'm going to be just like you. I'm going to help poor people like you do."

This made my day, my week, maybe my whole life.

By this time, a few of my friends were jumping on board the mission. Kate, my climbing partner on Everest, organized a fundraising event in San Francisco and I got the chance to meet her four children and family. (By the way, all of her fingers survived.) It was also a wonderful opportunity for us to compare notes on our experience and talk about how we were adjusting back home. We talked about how difficult it was to explain to anyone what it was like on the mountain and what it was like for us now. We admitted that we both startled easily and overreacted to loud noises, symptoms we knew were related to trauma. We each wondered when we would ever feel truly safe again.

CHAPTER 4

———— ∽ ————

Jeffrey: Meanwhile, Back at the Epicenter of Another Quake

May, 2015

I'D BEEN IN touch with Sara back home and I could tell she was suffering terribly, not just because of what she'd gone through on the mountain, but also because she felt helpless being so far away from what was now going on in Nepal. The place was an absolute wreck and becoming even more chaotic after the second big earthquake in the Everest region. Although there were daily aftershocks that were diffused throughout the country, the 7.3 trembler occurred pretty close to where we support a lot of our scholarship girls.

The Everest region is almost completely cut off from the rest of the country because the only practical access is via small planes that have to thread their way through a narrow valley. The territory is inhabited largely by the Sherpa tribe, originally migrants who settled the area from Siberia and what used to be called Tibet. They are known primarily for their prowess as mountain guides. To this day, the most accomplished climbers are of this heritage, following in the tradition of Tenzing Norgay, the first climber to successfully reach the summit of Everest with Sir Edmund Hillary.

Whereas 80% of the population of Nepal is Hindu and share similar traditions to those of neighboring India, the Sherpas are Buddhist and speak their own language that is similar to their Tibetan ancestors. They are a proud people who have learned to not only survive, but flourish in this mountainous region. Although the word "Sherpa" has become synonymous with "Himalayan guide," they are also self-sufficient farmers and entrepreneurs.

Most Sherpas share the same last name, which was a custom begun in the 1960s. Until that time, they just used first names that were determined by the day of the week they were born. For instance, our foundation is run by Pasang Sherpa; his wife's name is also Pasang because they were born on the same day of the week. Pasang likes to tell the story of his birth every time we pass the mountainous ridge where his mother was tending to a herd of yaks. She gave birth to him on the side of the slope while taking care of the animals and carried him down. Pasang was my first trekking guide many years ago, became interested in our work rescuing and supporting girls in potential danger, and eventually assumed responsibility for running our operation along with another friend, Babita Gurung, who we sponsored to complete her studies as a social worker.

Our medical team consisted of Pasang as our leader, Matt, our medic, Monet, a hospital administrator, Hill, who was operating as our pharmacist, Pema, one of our scholarship girls who was now a trauma nurse, and Chhusang, Pasang's daughter and our medical assistant. In addition to myself as the psychologist and trauma specialist, that was just about all the medical personnel available in the whole region. Except for Matt who had served as medical corpsman in the Marines, we were not exactly prepared to deal with the kinds of problems we would encounter after such a disaster. In fact, we were the first responders, and the only resources we had at our disposal were the nine duffel bags of medicine and supplies we'd been able to bring into the country. Since it had already been more than a week since the destruction occurred, we realized that infections, festering wounds, broken bones, and widespread trauma would be out of control.

Clueless and Overwhelmed

I've worked as a clinician for more than 40 years. I've lived and taught psychotherapy in a half-dozen countries and seen just about any kind of psychological problem that could possibly exist. I've written dozens of textbooks in the field, and more than 60 other books about psychological phenomena. I lecture all over the world and consider myself a qualified expert to deal with almost anyone who might show up in my office. The problem here was that I had no office, no support staff, and no access to any resources, books, online searches, or colleagues with whom I could refer cases.

Our medical team operating in a remote village in the Everest region. Back row: Jeffrey, Matt, Monet, Hill, Pasang Front row, center: Pema, Chhusang

Oh, did I mention that the reason I never had an interest in being a doctor was that I hate the sight of blood and physical suffering? I have never felt more helpless and clueless; I've never been so unprepared to do my job helping people. And yet here were hundreds of people streaming toward us whenever we would approach a village—bleeding, limping, sometimes being carried on someone's back. Most of these people had never in their lives seen a medical professional. I had already encountered this many times before in the remote areas in which our girls are located. I remember one time I was walking mindlessly along a trail when I saw this man running toward me down a mountainside. I could see his arm out-stretched above his head and I thought he was waving toward me. As he drew closer, I noticed that the hand was wrapped in a cloth which he pro-ceeded to hold out to me as if he wanted to greet me with a handshake. But right away I could see there was something terribly wrong. His fingers were swollen like sausages. There were huge, pus-filled blisters speckled all over, some of which had already burst open. The man was obviously in agony and was asking me for help.

Apparently, the people in this isolated region believed that any Westerner who might walk through was some kind of medical expert, or at least brought healing drugs with them. Before I could say anything, my guide explained that I was a doctor in America.

"Not *that* kind of doctor!" I tried to interrupt. But by then, they were talking back and forth and my guide explained that I could help him.

"This man, Sir," the guide explained. "He spilled boiling oil all over his hand. You must do something to help him."

"Me?"

"Sir, there is nobody else."

With no other choice I examined his hand, not at all sure what I should be looking for. It was obvious that his hand would soon become infected, if it wasn't already. So I pretended to be a doctor, trying my best to be calm and reassuring, even though I was trying my best not to vomit my lunch in disgust.

As I mentioned, I'm a psychologist, so most of my work takes place within the context of a caring relationship. So that's what I concentrated on first, looking into his eyes, telling him that he would be okay, that I could help him (lying through my teeth). I sat him down on a rock and looked into my pack, pulling out some bandages and antiseptic that I carried in my first aid kit. I carefully washed the blisters and applied the antiseptic, telling him first that he would feel excruciating pain. I told him that was a sign that the medication was working and healing his hand. I had no idea if that was true, but by now I had slipped into my hypnotic induction voice, soft, soothing, reassuring, all of it being (hopefully) translated by the guide. I bandaged the hand, first with gauze, then surgical tape, and then wrapped the whole package in duct tape as a kind of soft cast. Finally, I told him I had some very powerful medicine that would take the pain away and make him feel better. Actually, it was just aspirin, but I figured it was better than nothing.

This was my very first medical patient and I have no idea if I really helped him or not, or even if he survived. But I will never forget his grateful smile and hug as he walked back up the mountain to disappear into a cloud. I remembered this experience because I now realized that I would be dealing with similar issues times a hundred, or a thousand. I should have known what I'd be getting into as I was certainly no stranger to this part of the world. I remember going to a village in the Langtang Himalayan region, north of Kathmandu, where almost every single person had a huge goiter growing out the side of their neck because they only drank glacial water and had no iodine in their diets. I recall years ago being in places so isolated that it took four days just to walk to the nearest bus, and then another two days' journey to the nearest medical facility. If you developed appendicitis, you died. A compound fracture from a fall? No chance to survive. Complicated pregnancy? Except for the local midwife, no other help available.

I thought about all this as we carefully navigated a steep slope into a village where we could see everyone waiting for our arrival—word had spread that there were "doctors" coming to save them. Much of the trail was becoming increasingly difficult to navigate after the mudslides and avalanches had made their mark. In this part of the world, these narrow trekking routes were the interstate highways, the only way that supplies could be delivered by mule or yak. With the trails washed out, they were all completely cut off, which explained why we were the only aid workers around. And honestly, we weren't in the best shape trying to just survive the journey along these treacherous mountainsides, constantly looking over our shoulders for an escape route after the next quake that could occur any moment.

Some Rather Unusual Cases

I once wrote a book that was a collection of the most bizarre cases of the most famous therapists still alive at the time. And these were some doozies! The book's title was based on a friend's (and my coauthor's) case that involved a family in which the father died and the mother had him mummified to sit at the dining table for seven years. There were other cases in which the patient believed he was Rambo, or a Native American medicine man who wanted help having visions, or an 82-year-old, depressed prostitute, or a wealthy woman with an eating disorder who would only eat from garbage cans and dumpsters. So I wasn't exactly unfamiliar with the strangest variations of human behavior. Once again, my overconfidence led me to believe I could handle anything that came my way, just the sort of arrogance that lead many of us elder professionals to end up way in over our heads.

We set up our medical clinic in an open field so there was plenty of room for people to wait while we did our best to attend to as many as we could. In other locales we had been able to operate in a tent, or a schoolroom. In some cases, if the patient wasn't ambulatory, we'd make house calls. In each of them, Chhusang and I would set up shop in a separate area. One of our medical assistants was operating as our triage specialist, asking the long line of patients about their presenting symptoms, which usually included an infection and acute trauma along with hundreds of different medical issues that may or may not have resulted from the earthquake and its aftermath. There were terrible grief issues with so many people having lost family members. We could hear everyone coughing because of respiratory infections. And almost everyone was absolutely exhausted and desperate from sleep deprivation and post-traumatic stress symptoms that included nightmares, unrelenting anxiety, startle responses, pounding hearts, depression, hopelessness, and despair.

My first patient of the day qualified as perhaps the single most unusual case I've ever seen, or even heard of since the days of Freud. The woman had been referred to me after Matt, our doc, signaled to me that he couldn't help her. He shrugged, shook his head, and grinned at me, signaling that I could expect a lulu.

"Namaste," she said with her hands steepled into the traditional Nepali greeting, meaning roughly that the divine spirt in her honored the spirit within me.

I returned the greeting with a smile and asked how I could help her, after which she displayed her hand. Since I'm the psychologist on board, I wondered what I was supposed to do with it so I looked back over at Matt who just smiled and then went back to work on some surgery.

I learned through Chhusang's translations that she said her hand didn't work.

Okay, so what was I supposed to do for a broken hand?

"No," Chhusang explained, "her hand wasn't exactly broken. It just didn't work."

"What do you mean, her hand doesn't work?" I asked. I sent Chhusang over to Matt to find out what was going on and she returned to tell me that the woman's hand was paralyzed but he couldn't find anything medically wrong. The bones and ligaments were all perfectly functioning, but the appendage was completely numb.

I began to question the woman and learned that at the exact moment of the earthquake she had grabbed onto her mother's sleeve and held on as tightly as possible to steady them both as the building swayed back and forth, crumbling around them. Ever since then her hand had no sensation whatsoever.

"Uh-huh," I said, stalling as long as I could. *Now* what was I supposed to do? There was a lineup of impatient people waiting to get in to see me, growing longer every minute. I was used to doing a half dozen 50-minute therapy sessions during a typical day but during these clinics I was treating someone every few minutes. Time was racing along and, somehow, I was supposed to fix her problem; I had no idea where to begin. This was like one of those cases of hysterical trauma that Freud described among Victorian women a hundred years ago, a psychosomatic response to stress.

There was nothing in my fairly extensive repertoire of interventions that seemed to apply to this situation, so I remembered something I had once witnessed when working with indigenous healers in Africa where magic and mystery were so much a part of the rituals. Any self-respecting healer or witchdoctor would *never* resort to mere conversation for a cure, and this situation surely required something out of the box. So an idea came to me, a plan that struck me as both a little crazy but also entirely appropriate.

"I'm so glad you came to see me," I first reassured the woman with a smile, the whole time rubbing her numb hand with my own. "I *do* know how we can fix this problem."

She looked up at me hopefully, completely trusting my judgment. It's sad to say that Westerners in this part of the world command the kind of respect and awe that I could never experience elsewhere. And that would make my "placebo" cure even more powerful since it relied on faith and strong belief. It was discovered long ago that doctors can prescribe sugar pills for ailments and they can be antidotes just as powerful as those that are chemically active—*if* they are accompanied by appropriately persuasive reassurance. Faith and support are a strong part of *any* cure, which is why more than half of patients who consult with a physician don't actually have anything medically wrong—they just want a professional to tell them they'll be okay (with some kind of procedure or pill that may or may not have any actual medicinal properties).

With this in mind, I explained to the woman that she must follow my instructions carefully, to which she readily agreed.

"Are you certain?" I asked her once again just to increase the power of what I was about to tell her to do.

Again, she nodded.

"Okay, then, this is what you must do. Each morning when you awake I want your mother to massage your hand with warm oil for a minimum of fifteen minutes. Is that clear?"

Enthusiastic nod.

"Good. And I want her to do the same thing each night before you go to sleep."

She looked over to Chhusang who was staring at me with a look I couldn't interpret. I actually thought this would make some kind of sense in this culture because I remembered that during childbirth the women relatives of the expectant mother take turns rubbing warm, scented oil all over her body while they chant and sing.

"In addition," I continued, "I'm going to give you some very strong medicine that you are to take twice each day for the next three days, once in the morning before your mother massages your hand, and then before the evening hand rub. Is that clear?"

The woman smiled for the first time, "*Dhanyabahd, dheri, dheri dhanyabahd*," thanking me most effusively. I then proceeded to carefully count out the pills and place them in an envelope. They were actually just ibuprofen (Advil).

"So," Chhusang said to me, "what was *that* about?"

"I have no idea," I answered. "Bring in the next patient."

Like so many of the hundreds of people I treated during the next few weeks, I would never learn what happened to them, whether they lived or died, recovered or not. We were all just treading water.

A man brought his brother to see me who was obviously schizophrenic. The brother was clearly a danger to himself and others. He would throw rocks at people walking by, refuse to eat, and usually talked to himself most of the time, rarely responding to anyone else. He would not look at me the whole time we were together, nor would he respond to any question. He just rocked back and forth and giggled.

Again, what could I do? There were no hospitals. There were no medications for psychotic disorders, and when I told the brother that was the only thing that could help his brother, he started crying. Finally, I remembered that a Nepali psychiatrist friend was coming to Kathmandu in a few weeks and I promised to have her contact them for a consult.

A mother brought in her adult son who was severely depressed. As best as I could gather, he had been depressed for the past five years, but since the earthquakes he had become inconsolable. All he did was walk back and forth, refusing to acknowledge or speak to anyone. At least he would look at me and make occasional eye contact, but again, he needed meds to help him.

I saw a man with a head injury and vertigo who wanted me to listen and reassure him that he would regain cognitive functioning. An older woman presented memory problems, backaches, headaches that all seemed age appropriate but were more severe after the earthquake and sleeping outside on the ground for a week. I listened to a woman who was hearing voices, either of ghosts or God. Given that choice, I told her it must be God speaking to her because she was obviously very special. I asked her what God said to her but she either didn't know or wouldn't say.

I saw a 5-year-old girl, then a 6-year-old boy, one after the other, both presenting the same symptoms of frequent urination and bed wetting. Well, not exactly, since they have no beds sleeping outside. All of us were sleeping outside, so backaches, headaches, and neck aches were commonplace, if not from the hard ground then from the unrelenting stress of the earth constantly shaking.

One After Another

I had already seen four families in a row without a break and my energy was faltering. Many cases were so similar: one or more of the children had a headache or stomachache or sleep problem and the parents were worried. Or an adult was hyper-vigilant and over-reactive to any noise or movement, unable to sleep or eat. Or some preexisting medical condition like hypertension or heart problems were now far more serious. There were so many people wanting attention and care that eventually I started seeing them in small groups, a half-dozen or more at a time. I taught them a rudimentary form of deep breathing, a simplified form of self-talk, but mostly explained and normalized their reactions as typical of trauma symptoms and chronic, unrelenting fear.

Since this was a region where many of our scholarship girls lived, on occasion a familiar face would show up to say hello or report on how they were doing. Almost all of them asked where Sara was, and I explained what happened on Everest and that she was at home but would be returning to see them soon.

I spent time with an older girl, one of our scholarship students who wanted to attend medical school next year, but whose father thought that it was time for her to be married now that she was 18. He insisted girls didn't belong in school and tried to sabotage her studies as much as he could. What should she do? Could she disobey her father and pursue her studies? Or should she follow her dreams and risk being disowned? I had spoken to her a few months earlier when I was in Nepal with several of my counseling students and had told her that the choice was hers and promised that if she wanted to continue medical training, we would provide alternative housing and support for her. I had directed my counseling students to talk to her, and one student, Karla, shared her own story of emigrating from Mexico when she was 12, unable to speak English, leaving everything behind, and also showing resolve to be the first in her family to ever attend university, much less graduate school. This seemed to strongly impact the girl and now I was following up with her.

I was running out of energy—and hope—when a distraught mother approached me with her reluctant 10-year-old son in tow. She explained that her son refused to eat and she was concerned about his health. He actually looked reasonably healthy to me, hardly anorectic. She was one of the few people I met who had actually consulted with doctors and they ruled out any physical problem, diagnosing an eating disorder. This was something I'd not yet encountered in a country where the vast majority of the population doesn't have enough food to eat.

After a bit of questioning, I discovered that he was reasonably normal and happy in other ways, the family was intact and all healthy. Yes, their home had been damaged and they were living outside, but they planned to move back inside if there were no further quakes in the next few days.

This tent operated as our medical clinic in an open field where people had assembled after their homes were destroyed.

Besides, this refusal to eat began long before the earthquakes. Again I felt the pressure to do something, fix this problem, especially since by now I was working inside a barricaded schoolroom to keep the crowd of waiting patients from fighting to get inside.

I told the boy I had a test for him and wondered if he would pass. He looked intrigued so I told him that I bet I could find something that he might like to eat. He barely looked at me but I could see the beginning of a smile. I pulled out a Snickers bar and handed it to him. Out of pure obstinacy, he shrugged and passed it to his mother, pretending he wasn't interested. He looked back at me defiantly, the glimpse of a smile now gone.

"What *do* you like to eat?" I asked him.

He didn't bother to answer. Just shook his head.

"What about smoothies?" I remembered his mother said that they'd visited Kathmandu before.

For the first time, he nodded his head in the affirmative, or rather waggled it back and forth in that characteristic Nepali way that is both an indistinct, yes and no, and also maybe.

"What about KFC?" I always found it interesting that the single busiest, most popular restaurant in Kathmandu was fried chicken from the colonel.

Another nod.

"Kabobs?"

Again a nod.

"So, what *don't* you like to eat?" This was not like any eating disorder I'd ever heard of.

He whispered something I couldn't hear. "Say that again," I prompted him.

"*Dahl baht.*"

"I see." And now I *did* see. Most Nepali people eat rice and lentils for both meals of the day, every day, even when they are provided other choices. It is perhaps the single most nutritious meal that the human body could metabolize and provides a cheap and efficient source of protein and energy. It turned out he really didn't have an eating disorder at all, he just didn't like *dahl baht* but he *loved* fast food. I instructed the mother to vary his diet, recognizing that this might be my first sure-fire cure.

My head hurt with concentration. I desperately needed a break and to use the toilet. Before I could get out of my chair, a tiny girl was carried into the room by a man, accompanied by a woman I assumed was the girl's mother. They were followed by the principal of the local school and Pasang Sherpa, our leader and guide.

Since confusion was my usual state of mind, I just sat and waited for the drama to unfold. I wondered what could possibly surprise me next.

"This is Pramisa," Pasang said to me, pointing to this absolutely adorable girl who was looking around the room, studying all of us carefully. "She is three years old."

I nodded, waiting. Pasang and the principal explained to me that the man and woman were her aunt and uncle.

"Where are her parents?" I asked.

Everyone looked at one another after the translation. Her mother was at the hospital. "She is dressed in white," the uncle said.

"She is dressed in white?" I repeated, now completely confused.

"Yes," Pasang agreed. "Her husband, the girl's father, died yesterday. He was hit on the head during the last earthquake. He was in the hospital and he died. The mother is with the body, dressed in white as she is required. This girl, she doesn't have a father and we haven't told her yet."

I looked at this little girl, Pramisa, and she was smiling and playing with a stuffed animal I had just given her. My heart just broke. I could feel myself losing control, tears running down my cheeks, and so I excused myself for a moment and walked out of the room to regain my composure. Were we now going to tell this 3-year-old that her father was never coming home? I had already seen and done so much, but this I could not do. But I knew I had to go back in the room.

Once I was back in my chair, Pasang asked if we might offer this girl a scholarship, support her now that she had lost her father and her home. They had no money, no place to live, and no way to earn an income. The mother would spend a year in mourning and that would be her job.

I thought to myself how fate had put me in this place, at this moment in time. My chest hurt. I felt so flooded with emotion from all the accumulated stress, all the stories I had heard, all the people I had seen. I had felt so helpless at times, so inadequate to provide the help and support that everyone needed. And now I was given this gift: I could save this child, literally save her life by agreeing to provide her with a scholarship so she could have an education and a future.

I could barely speak, but I nodded my head, once, twice, then up and down so vigorously everyone looked at me curiously. "Yes, of course," I finally spoke aloud. I looked at the aunt and uncle and told them that although this was a terrible tragedy, I would do everything in my power to make certain that Pramisa was provided an education, to go as far as she could in life, maybe even to become a doctor or an engineer, professions that were rarely possible for girls.

Then I fled the room, went into the toilet, shut the door, and started sobbing. In fact, I am crying now as I try to tell this story. And things got so much worse for her. A few days later I was told that a pot of boiling water was spilled all over her neck and back, sending her to the hospital for treatment of her burns. The little girl is in a complete daze, not understanding this cascade of terrible things that are happening to her, one after another.

A few months after her father died, and after she had been horribly burned, Pramisa received a scholarship to support her education for the rest of her life.

Tag Team: It's Sara's Turn Again

After several more weeks of this constant pressure, 13-hour workdays, sleep deprivation, and my own vicarious trauma from everything I'd seen and done, I was absolute toast. My aging body was breaking down. I don't weigh much to begin with and I'd lost so much weight my clothes were literally falling off. I'd had enough. I needed to refuel and recover. In fact, this would be one of my last visits to Nepal before retiring and turning over the reins to our new team, which included Sameer, our new President, Patrice, a colleague at another university, and Sara, who would now be serving on our Board of Directors along with several other friends, Maryellen and Jeremy. I'd been spending every winter break in Nepal for the past 15 years, missing the holidays with my family, and I just couldn't endure the discomforts and stress much longer. I planned to return again in a few months, perhaps for the last time, so I was turning more and more responsibility over to Sameer, Sara and others.

This visit had been among the most difficult and painful experiences of my life. Besides seeing all the devastation and suffering, I felt so disturbed seeing so many of our girls who seemed to be giving up hope. I had known many of them most of their lives. I had spent time with their families, visiting their homes and classrooms. Now all that was gone and I could see them squatting in tents perched in the mud.

I knew we'd done a lot of good. I also realized that the people in Nepal are among the most resilient in the world. They'd have to be after years of political instability and corruption, natural disasters, and government inaction, yet they *still* endured and tried to rebuild their lives—and did so with apparent good cheer. Their homes and schools had been destroyed, teachers disappeared. They were making do with almost nothing while many of the current politicians were becoming wealthier from bribes and theft. Most people would just shrug, as if that's just the way things are, the way they'll always be. The Nepali people have taught me so much about the courage to rebuild their lives, even when things appear so hopeless.

After so much time has passed, my heart still hurts. I still sometimes have trouble sleeping and have been unable to gain weight back. I know this is the result of so-called "compassion fatigue," as well as my primary trauma of surviving a major earthquake and dozens of smaller ones. I know it is the result of working insane hours and seeing so much devastation and despair, so much sickness. I know that what we had done was just a drop in the bucket compared to the millions of people who still need help, needed tents and food and water, needed support. But after a lifetime devoted to service, a life dedicated to teaching and helping others, I am certain that everything I had ever done, everything I had ever prepared for, was to be there when people needed me most.

CHAPTER 5

— ⚭ —

Sara: Going Beyond Myself

2012

IT HAD BEEN over 15 years since I first moved to the United States from Iran with my family during a time of great turmoil. Yes, I know there *always* seems to be a certain amount of turbulence in that part of the world, nations feuding with one another, Sunnis versus Shia, clergy versus royal families—it seems never-ending. We managed to escape the chaos to make a better life for ourselves the way so many other immigrants came to this country for sanctuary and better opportunities.

There had been a series of student protests against the Iranian government crackdown on more freedoms, leading to the arrest of more than 4,000 people, with dozens of others murdered in the streets or tortured in dungeons. During this time I was a student studying at university in Tehran and I tried to remain as invisible as possible. So far my family had been waiting 13 years for visas to leave the country and I didn't want to take the risk that anything I might do would ruin our chances. I had been arrested a few times, once because the skin on my arm was showing after I rolled up the sleeves of my dress, and the second time because I had been studying with a male student to whom I wasn't married.

I lived constantly in fear of getting in trouble. My family was not religious, nor particularly observant, but I'd been told over and over again at school ever since I was a child that a girl would go to Hell if she did not always cover herself. Women had to ask men permission for everything, especially to ever leave the country, which was my dream. Although I was studying engineering, I knew that I'd never have the opportunity to work as a real professional in Iran; my parents approved of my studies because they thought it would make me more independent.

Once we were finally granted permission to leave Iran, I started dreaming about America and all the things I would be allowed to do there that I could never do at home. Although my parents and siblings settled in Arizona, I had always wanted to attend the University of California, Los Angeles to study electrical engineering. I thought the campus was the most beautiful place I'd ever seen with the brick buildings, the diversity of students, and the highest academic standards. The people on campus were so many different colors and spoke so many languages. I'd never seen anything like this. I applied and was accepted; however, I discovered I was not prepared for the many adjustments I would have to make to reach my goal.

First of all, the university wouldn't accept any of my three previous years of study so I had to start over again. Secondly, I had learned English in Tehran with a British accent and people sometimes had a hard time understanding me, as I did them. The customs were so different too. In the Persian culture it is common for girls to hold hands when they walked around, but I remember reaching for another student's hand as we were strolling to class and she pulled away, accusing me of being a lesbian. In addition, students spent so much time in bars and I hadn't yet ever tasted alcohol. Girls wore tank tops, shorts, and revealing clothes, another thing to which I was unaccustomed.

Throughout my time at UCLA I worked hard to achieve the highest grades, not only to make my family proud, but also so I could build a good life for myself. It was all about wanting things that I could never have back in Iran. I wanted to be able to support myself without depending on a man. I wanted a nice car. I wanted a nice house. Eventually I wanted a husband, too, and maybe a few kids. It was all about wanting without almost any thought about what would truly make me happy. I could earn the best grades, get the best job, maybe even become a professor and teach engineering, but I started to wonder if that was what would really make me satisfied.

I remember I had just finished my last set of final exams and was feeling especially pleased that my grades were absolutely perfect, straight-A's that semester. And then the thought hit me that maybe this was it, that I'd already gone as far as I could go. Maybe it's the way a champion athlete feels once she achieves stardom at such a young age. How can you possibly top that except to live on the laurels of the past? All of a sudden my mood plummeted and I thought to myself there's just *got* to be something more than this to life, more than just academic achievement.

I had been talking to friends about this specific life challenge when one of them suggested that I check out a communication and leadership program that is known all over the world. I started attending classes, just to diversify my life in some ways. I'd always been good at math and science and technical subjects, which is why I chose to study engineering. You've got to understand how unusual this was for a girl from Iran where such opportunities are very limited. Maybe that's why I wanted to break this mold, to prove that women really could do almost anything men could do. Although it seemed easy for me to master the intricacies of multivariate calculus, electromagnetism, digital signal processing, and electronic circuit analysis, there was definitely some work I needed to do with regard to my interpersonal and speaking skills. I wanted more for my life than sitting in a laboratory designing and testing circuit boards to optimize their speed and power usage.

Hiding Under the Table

There was a reason I was more than a little bit annoyed by the control and power of men in my life: my father used to terrify me—and everyone else in the household. He was an angry and unhappy man who decided to make everyone else miserable to keep him company.

Actually he wasn't my real father who had died four months before I was born in the war with Iraq. My mother never told me anything about him or explained why my last name was different from my siblings. She had married her second husband when I was two years old, so he was the only father I had ever known. I knew from the earliest age that he often didn't much like having me around.

I remember one day when I was 6 years old, playing under the dining room table, crawling over the chairs and climbing between them. Maybe this was the very beginning of my climbing career because I loved to explore and climb things. I had carefully arranged all my dolls and stuffed animals on a blanket beside the table, covering them with another blanket while they took an afternoon nap. Some of my other toys were scattered around the floor.

I heard the front door creak open and then slam shut so hard I could feel the vibrations. "Nasim," I heard my father yell at my mother, "what the hell is going on around here? The house is a mess. What were you doing all day while I've been working so hard?"

My mother was in the kitchen preparing dinner so she didn't get the full brunt of his rage. But I did while cowering under the table, fearful he would punish me. One of his punishments was to lock me in the storage room for hours, but I had already discovered a way to manage that by hiding some of my favorite books in there so I actually looked forward to the solitude.

"I'm sorry, Babak," my mother said, wiping her hands on a towel. "I didn't know you were coming home so early."

"This house is not clean! It's a mess. Look at all the shit around here," he said, pointing to my stuff scattered on the floor. I was still hiding in the shadow of the table.

"Babak," my mother tried to explain, "I was just. . ."

I heard a loud smack and saw my mother fall to the floor after he'd hit her. She started crying and then he walked outside to smoke a cigarette. My mother could see me under the table and that made her even more fearful. "Quick, run to the public phone and tell your uncle to come quickly. Otherwise, I. . . I don't know. . ."

I nodded my head in understanding and my mother placed a small coin in my hand to make the call. She repeated my uncle's phone number several times so I could repeat it back to her. Then I ran as fast as I could out the door, hoping my father would not catch me.

Because I was so little, I had to climb up to reach the phone booth. I could barely grasp the phone so when I tried to put the coin in the slot it became stuck and I couldn't push it in. I was just so scared that something would happen to my mother while I was away that all I could think to do was rush home to try and save her.

My mother was still huddled on the floor a few minutes later, holding her hand to the side of her face. The memories of this day are all muddled together because they merge with so many others just like it when we all lived in fear of my father's temper. We all understood that he'd lived through some very difficult times and, strangely, I could never bring myself to blame him for scaring me so much. It just made me even more determined to never allow a man to control my life when I got older. And I think this is one reason why I feel such a close connection to the girls in Nepal who face similar situations.

Although in school, and at home, I tried my best to remain as unobtrusive as possible, I was actually quite rebellious when nobody was looking. It was my way of fighting back. I'd sneak out of the house to play soccer with the boys in my neighborhood. I visited places I was not supposed to go. Every time my father would hit or punish me, it only made me stronger: I would not allow him—or anyone—to defeat me. My mother had always told me that education was the way out of this trap, so that was one area where I made sure to always excel, almost without half trying. Education was equal to freedom for me, and that's why I like to help Nepali girls to get an education and to be independent.

I realized that nothing I could ever do would please my father. But as I grew older, I wanted so badly to put all these bad memories behind me. I had already understood that, in so many ways, he was doing the best he could, given his own wounds. Eventually I reached a place where I could forgive him and realize my own role in our conflicts and disagreements. I had by this time started taking courses in personal growth and public speaking, all aimed at improving my self-confidence. Already I could feel myself changing the way I think about things and letting some things go that were still bothersome.

After I graduated from the university, I immediately got a job as a test engineer working on power management systems for mobile phones, and then working on software for autopilot systems in airplanes. I was now a professional engineer, the pride of my family, but still it didn't feel nearly enough.

Beyond the Impossible

Choosing science and engineering as my fields of study limited my exposure to so many other aspects of life about which I was completely unaware. So perhaps it isn't that surprising that I was immediately impacted by what I was learning in the leadership program I was attending to improve my interpersonal skills. I learned to let go of some of my past resentments and think differently about some of the experiences that continued to haunt me. I eventually found—or made—the time to continue my personal growth as well. I signed up for another seminar in which we were required to make a commitment and public declaration of an ambitious goal that would be transformative for our lives. We were asked to reach for something so big, so huge, that it might seem impossible, but nevertheless a dream that excited us. This wasn't just about losing a few pounds or quitting your job and joining the circus—or maybe that *was* an option—but we were encouraged to choose something beyond our imaginations.

Frankly, nothing immediately came to mind; I just sat there feeling stuck. In order to fulfill some dream, first you have to have one, and I was drawing a complete blank. First, I thought about taking a dance or painting class: Nope, too easy. Then I considered going on for a Ph.D. in electrical engineering: that was harder, for sure, but I could still do that without too much difficulty. I considered starting my own business, but I'd already heard other participants declare that one. Besides, I wasn't motivated to make a lot of money. I already owned a car and I had an apartment that was a dump, but it was still mine. I didn't really need anything else.

I thought about maybe writing a book. But what would I write about? I hadn't yet done anything worth recording. I always wanted to open a wellness center, but that didn't seem that impossible either. I needed to think of something truly spectacular.

And then it hit me as I was listening to the chatter around me in the room. I could hear echoes of conversation in which other participants were talking to one another about their plans. Some were bouncing ideas off one another to test them out.

Behind me I could hear two people talking. "I think I'm going to. . . but I have this friend, Suzanne, she went to Nepal to go trekking."

"Trekking in Nepal?" the other one said, and started giggling. "Isn't that kind of dangerous? I mean they've got avalanches and I think there's some kind of civil war going on."

"No, seriously, she went trekking in the Himalayas and went all the way to Everest Base Camp. She said it was amazing. It was really hard but totally worth it."

I know this sounds crazy, but in that moment I thought to myself, "That's it! But I'm not going to just trek to Base Camp, I'm going to climb Mount Everest!" Before I could stop myself I blurted out my goal to the group. I felt giddy with the power of my declaration and basked in the attention from everyone in the room. I could see that I trumped all the other goals and I could see the leader grinning, giving me two thumbs up.

What makes this even more ridiculous is that I'd never been climbing, or even hiking in my life—I'd never even been camping before! I realized that even when we went on family picnics I refused to touch anything because I was terribly afraid of insects. I remembered one time I had taken off my shoes to walk in the river and I stepped on a huge bug. I could feel the crunchy sound under my foot and screamed hysterically, insisting that we go home right away so I could wash off my feet.

If my lack of experience in Nature wasn't enough of an obstacle, another problem was that I absolutely hated cold weather. Even in

Southern California, land of eternal sunshine, I would complain whenever the temperature dipped below 70 degrees. I'd also never been on a real mountain before, and even the prospect of snow was somewhat of a mystery to me. I didn't own a single piece of clothing or equipment that would be appropriate for such an adventure. In addition, I didn't exactly consider myself in particularly good shape. I worked out at the gym a few days each week, but nothing serious. If our leader truly wanted us to pick something that was beyond impossible, I sure delivered that. But *now* what was I going to do? I looked around the room with everyone staring at me, but now I couldn't let them down. They actually expected me to *do* this.

Instruction Manual for Climbing Everest

If I thought I had gotten some strange looks when I announced my plan to those at the seminar, I hadn't anticipated the reactions I'd get from my family and friends when I told them what I had in mind.

"That's pretty funny," one friend said, thinking I was kidding. "So, what you are guys doing this weekend?"

"I just told you what I'm doing and you just ignored me."

He just laughed. "You idiot! That's for rich people."

I didn't tell my family at all as I knew that would be a hopeless cause only leading to more grief and discouragement. So I decided to keep it all a secret, a skill that I'd been trained to do from the earliest age. Even my husband, Matt, thought this was just a passing fad that would eventually run its course, and his best strategy was just to indulge me. I couldn't exactly disagree with him, considering that I had already learned on the Internet that the climb itself would take two months and I couldn't imagine living in the cold or being away from Matt that long.

Okay, so maybe I would have reacted much the same way if someone without any experience, training, or even any previous interest in mountaineering, all of a sudden proclaimed she was going to attempt one of the most difficult and dangerous climbs in the world. The first thing I had done when I got home was to Google, "How to climb Mount Everest," as if there would be instructions I could follow. After all, I'm a computer geek and engineer; I'm pretty good at following directions.

The first thing I learned was that something like one in four people who attempt the summit end up dying in the process. Hmmm. That wasn't very encouraging. I read further to discover there were more than a dozen bodies still frozen up there that they couldn't pry loose, as well as various body parts and artifacts of those who tried to get to the top and failed.

I'm not one to be dissuaded easily—some have called me stubborn. I once decided to travel to Egypt by myself. I had read about how many women traveling alone had been kidnapped, some of them even taken in order to extract their kidneys and other organs for sale on the black market. Friends kept telling me to take a man with me for protection, but I was sure I could do this on my own. And once again, I didn't ever want to depend on a man for anything.

Those closest to me knew quite well that they would be better off just not saying anything to try and talk me out of my plan—or it would just make me more determined to prove them wrong. During my initial search for information about how to climb Everest, I noticed there was one company that appeared to be mentioned frequently as one of the major expedition leaders, so I simply called them on the phone.

"Good morning, International Climbing" I heard a voice answer.

"Hi, I have a question for you."

"Yes, of course."

"How do I climb Mount Everest?"

"Let me transfer you. Please hold."

As I was waiting I could feel my heart pounding. I couldn't believe I was actually doing this, or even thinking about doing this.

"So," another voice picked up, this time a guy who I assumed was one of their guides, "I understand you are interested in one of our Everest expeditions."

"Yes, so what can you tell me and what do I need to do?"

"Well, first of all, tell me about your previous climbing experience."

"My climbing experience?"

"Yeah, which 6,000 meter summits have you already done?"

I did the math in my head. Six thousand meters was over 19,000 feet, 19,685 to be precise. And I guess he wasn't referring to the time I had spent at altitude in an airplane. "Well," I admitted right away, "actually I've never been climbing before."

I could hear the guy laughing and it made me angry.

"Alright then, why don't you start with Mount Whitney? It's in California, the highest peak in the continental United States. You can do it as a day hike. Try that and then maybe give us a call back."

Click.

If this guide thought he was discouraging me, he was wrong. Now I had a place to begin. I was so excited that I immediately started reading about Whitney and how to climb it, which routes were possible, and what equipment I'd need. I read about people's experiences on their blogs and their comments and realized that this would be a lot more than a stroll in the park. But still, it was *only* 14,500 feet and Everest was literally *double* that height. So how hard could it be?

This was in the middle of winter and there would likely be tons of snow on the mountain. Almost everyone who attempts the summit waits until the middle of July when the trails are clear, but there was no way I was going to wait to put my plan into action. Besides, I was thinking there's snow on Everest, isn't there? This would be even better training for the real thing.

The next day I showed up at REI, a local outdoor store, and walked up to the first salesperson I could find, a young guy with shoulder-length hair and a full, beard. He looked like the kind of guy who might know a thing or two about climbing mountains. "Excuse me, I was wondering. . . I mean, I have a question."

He looked up from folding fleece sweaters on a table, obviously a little annoyed with my interruption, but he quickly recovered and remembered to smile. "Sure, what can I help you find?"

"Well," I explained, all in a rush, "I'm planning on climbing Mount Whitney in a few weeks. I don't have any gear for something like that and I was wondering if you could help me?"

"You want to climb Whitney?"

I nodded.

"Now? You want to climb Whitney now?"

"Uh-huh." I gave him my best smile.

"You do know it's winter this time of year? The temperature is like, below zero, with 30-mile-per-hour winds. And snow. Lots of snow."

"That's perfect," I answered. "Because I'm planning on climbing Everest, so this will be similar conditions."

"Lady, that's just not possible. Is this a joke or something?"

Now I was becoming more than a little annoyed. Nobody was taking me seriously. I think even Matt believed that once I tried this out a few times, I'd come to my senses and do something else. But I was determined and I think this salesman saw that look in my eyes.

"Okay, okay," he said, holding his hand out in a gesture of a surrender after having spent 10 minutes telling me all the reasons why I couldn't and shouldn't attempt such a stupid thing. "I'll tell you what you'd need for something like this, but I've got to warn you, what you're thinking about is really dangerous. I've been climbing for a lot of years and I'd never do something like this during the winter."

The baskets in the store were too small for everything I'd need, so we found a shopping cart and filled it to the brim with a lot more stuff than I could possibly have anticipated—wool underwear, fleece tops, layers of clothing, boots, crampons, gloves, facemask, and a waterproof, breathable shell jacket that was insanely expensive. We added a backpack, water bottles, a sleeping bag and pad, water purification tablets, and all kinds of other stuff. "Oh yeah, you'll need a pair of sunglasses."

"Got those already," I said with a grin, pointing to the pair perched on my head.

He shook his head with worry. "Look, lady. Even though it's winter, the sun is intense and reflects off the snow. It will burn you to a crisp and probably give you snow blindness." When he saw my confused look, he explained, "You need the kind of polarized glacier glasses to protect your eyes." Again he just shook his head. I had to be the most memorable customer he'd seen in a long time. In fact, I'm pretty sure he's *still* talking about me. Eddie and I eventually became friends. He was a rock climbing instructor and I eventually took a few of his classes.

Once I had all the equipment and supplies organized and assembled, my next task was to begin training. So I filled up my pack with all the stuff, added a few books in there for more weight, and headed off to the gym to start walking on a treadmill. This wasn't as simple as I thought because, at first, the gym wouldn't let me into the place with my pack. "We have rules against this sort of thing."

"Against *what* sort of thing?" I asked. The receptionist wouldn't budge, so I had to join another fitness club that had a more relaxed policy.

I was surprised that walking with the pack was so difficult, much heavier than I thought it would be, and several times I almost fell over backwards. I've always been in pretty good shape. I was on the swim team in high school, but maybe that wasn't such a big deal because most of the girls in my school didn't know how to swim and their parents would never allow them to wear a bathing suit even if they did. Still, I was dedicated enough that I'd swim laps for hours every single day during practices. It was just this kind of self-discipline that led me to try my first hiking experiences on some of the local mountains. This wasn't going to be so hard after all.

It occurred to me that mountaineering expeditions always have teams of climbers who work together, so I needed to recruit my own members. I started calling everyone I knew to invite them to go with me on my expedition, starting with my best friend, Pari.

"Ah, gee, thanks for the invitation," she answered without hesitation. "But I *definitely* have plans that weekend."

"But I didn't mention which weekend we were going yet. I just told you I was going to do this and asked if you wanted to join me."

"Okay, then, you're right," Pari begged off. "But this kind of thing just isn't my thing, if you know what I mean."

I did know what she meant. I guess stepping back, it did seem a little outlandish asking my friends to climb the highest peak in the country—in the winter—without any prior experience. But I'd seen photos of people at the summit and some of them didn't look like they were in particularly good shape. How hard could it be?

Finally, one of my friends mentioned someone he knew, Jim, who was an experienced climber. Maybe he'd go with me? I could tell he was just trying to get me off his back, but I appreciated the gesture. So I called Jim and he accepted my invitation—my first team member! "Sure," he agreed, "I'll go with you. I totally support you all the way to the top of Everest." He even assembled a group of his climbing friends who would join us to climb to the top of Whitney.

It was the middle of December when we prepared to leave. I tried my pack on after being loaded with all my stuff, noting that it seemed a *lot* heavier than when I had been practicing on a treadmill. That's the first time I considered that this adventure might be a little over my head. Those creeping thoughts became a lot more than a whisper when we first started up the trail in the deep snow. I hadn't slept the night before at our starting point that was already at 10,000 feet. I'd already mentioned I'd never been camping before. I couldn't sleep. My heart was pounding in my chest from the altitude and that scared me. I kept hearing noises in the middle of the night that I thought might be bears threatening to eat me (I didn't even realize, at that point, that bears hibernate in the winter.). The worst part of all was pooping and peeing in the wilderness. Being a woman from the Middle East, I wasn't exactly prepared for going to the toilet "in public," and I was too scared to wander too far into the woods because I was afraid that something might eat me.

To make matters worse, my friend Jim had a bad headache and nausea from the altitude, and we hadn't even started climbing yet. I was so, so disappointed that we'd come this far and now we had to turn back before we even started. I told Jim to wait for me so I could at least go a little bit up the trail. Once I was alone, I started to talk to the mountain. "Hello, there, Whitney," I began, feeling more than a little foolish. "I just want to let you know that I have to leave now." I stopped to look up to where I thought the summit might be. "But I promise I'm coming back. Real soon."

I was extremely frustrated that my first mountaineering experience took the form of basically peeing in the woods. But it took two more months before I could convince anyone else to go with me, and I knew it wasn't the sort of thing I could do alone for the first time. It was the middle of February, even colder than before, when another friend and I prepared to make the trip. And this time I was absolutely determined to get to the top no matter what. I'd already lost time in my planned training schedule. Unfortunately, at the very last moment, my friend backed out saying he had to take care of some business. I don't know if I believed him or not, but it didn't matter—I was going on my own.

Just before I left on the trip, I was sitting in a restaurant with my closest friend and I confided in her that I was terrified. "Look," I tried to reassure her (and myself), "I'm not stupid, and I don't have a death wish, but I made a promise to myself in front of a whole room full of people and all my friends, and I just have to keep my word. It's a matter of honor."

Of course she tried to talk me out of going, but she could also tell there was no argument that she, or anyone else, could muster that would persuade me otherwise: I was going—and that was that!

"I realize this is very dangerous," I told her. "I could die up there alone. But if anything happens to me, I just want you to know that I will have died doing something that was among the most important things in my life. I've just *got* to find out if I can do this, and I can't wait any longer." Before we said goodbye, as a last gift she gave me the "doggie bag" filled with our leftovers from the meal, a few slices of pizza and some buffalo wings.

A Nudge from the Universe

The morning of the climb I woke up to a huge snowfall. The road was closed in and out of Whitney trailhead but I still wouldn't let that stop me. I continued on in my car, slipping and sliding until I ended up stuck in a ditch. Foiled again! I was in the middle of nowhere, with no chance of anyone around to help me. So you can imagine my surprise when two guys walked up to me wondering what the hell I was doing out there in the middle of winter. When I told them I was on my way to climb Whitney, for reasons I still don't understand, they just nodded their heads like that made perfect sense and proceeded to push me out of the ditch to continue on my way. It's like they were angels sent to help and support me. I still believe that when you want something badly enough, when there's something you just *have* to do, the forces of the universe show up to give you a nudge. In my case, quite literally.

Once arriving at the trailhead, I looked around and noticed that not only was I the only human inhabitant in the vicinity, but from looking at the snow-covered landscape, it didn't look like anyone had been around for a while.

I geared up and settled the backpack on my shoulders loaded with all my supplies, two liters of water, including the leftover pizza and buffalo wings, which I realized weren't exactly "regulation" nutrition for this sort of expedition. I started up before I got too cold, and maybe that's why I immediately developed leg cramps. I thought that maybe that was a sign, a warning, that I should turn around, but I realized if I gave up now, my whole plan would collapse.

It had taken a solid hour just to walk from the car to the trailhead in the deep snow. With every step, I'd sink up to my thighs, so I worried I might get stuck and not be able to move. I was also concerned that all the streams were frozen, leading me to wonder how I'd replenish my water supply. It was eerily quiet, not a sound except my labored breathing.

I forced myself to continue upward and after another mile or two, my muscles settled into an almost comfortable cadence. I climbed and climbed all day long, finally reaching a spot to set up camp for the night just as it started to get dark. It was getting really cold now that the sun had fallen behind the mountains and I was losing visibility. The whole landscape was blanketed with snow. The only relatively dry spot I could find to make camp was on top of a flat rock that was slightly tilted.

The next order of business was to resupply my water since I finished the two liters on the way up and I knew the only way to starve off altitude sickness was to keep myself hydrated (Eddie, the REI sales guy, kept telling me that over and over.). After laying out all my gear and arranging my sleeping bag, I trounced down to the lake below me, which was frozen solid. It was a good thing I had an ice ax with me, wasn't it?

I chopped a hole in the ice large enough to slip the bottles underneath to refill them, feeling my hands freezing instantly from the bitter cold. As I walked back to my camp, I kept flexing my fingers over and over to regain some measure of circulation. It occurred to me that the bottles of water themselves would likely freeze in these temperatures within hours if I didn't take precautions, so I put both of them at the bottom of my bag, knowing my body heat would keep them in a relatively liquid state.

Actually, that's a lie. I learned that much, much later. At this point all I could think about was that there was no way I wanted to leave my sleeping bag during the night. I figured that keeping them in my bag would be much more convenient. It was an excellent idea, except for one little thing—it turned out that my hand had been so numb after I extricated them from the frozen lake that I didn't completely screw the top onto one of the bottles, which proceeded to drench my bag. I reached inside the bag to try and take the leaking bottle out, and in so doing, I stepped on my sleeping pad, made a hole in it, and it immediately flattened.

Oh, did I happen to mention that I decided *not* to bring a tent with me on the climb in order to save some weight in my bag? So here I was sitting on a rock on top of a wet sleeping bag, with the temperature plummeting and the wind starting to blow furiously. I wasn't sure if I was shaking now because of the bitter cold or my own terror knowing that I was in deep, deep trouble. "So," I said to myself out loud, "*this* is how people die out here." Then I burst into tears, huddling myself into a ball.

The best I can figure, I sat there sobbing for about 20 minutes, eventually awaking from the stupor when the wind started kicking up snow into my face. I didn't seem to have much time left so I crawled inside my wet sleeping bag, which was only a little better than moving from a freezer into a refrigerator. I took out my phone and turned on the video to record my last words.

I later watched the recording and, even now, I feel such shame at my cowardice. I was this blubbery mess, tears running down my cheeks until they seemed to freeze in place, my voice barely audible above the roaring of the wind.

0:02 / 0:21

With a wet sleeping bag, no tent, below zero temperatures, and driving wind and snow, I didn't think I would last through the night on Mt. Whitney, so I recorded a video to say a tearful goodbye to my family and friends.

"I'm so, so sorry. So sorry. I shouldn't have come here. I shouldn't be here alone. Everyone was right. I have no business doing this. Not. . . not. . .just not a good idea. But too late. I wish. . .I wish I didn't do this. I wish. . ." And then it abruptly stopped.

But then a funny thing happened. It's like my brain got plugged back in or something. I could hear this voice talking to me, saying "You don't have to die here."

All My Fears

All of a sudden, the stuff I'd been reading about mountaineering came back to me. "First of all, I've got to quit whining. Then I've got to get some food in me right away and start moving to get some heat back into my body before it's too late." Then I remembered the buffalo wings and pizza, which sounds pretty damn good when you are stuck on top of a freezing mountain in the middle of nowhere. It took more than two hours of running in place, to get some feeling back into my limbs. By this time I needed to rest after having spent the previous nine hours climbing all day. I kept telling myself, "Don't fall asleep, don't fall asleep," or I knew it would be all over for me. I had to try and stay awake all night or I'd freeze to death for sure in the frigid bag that was sopping wet.

I must have dozed off because about two in the morning I felt some-one—or something—touching my bag. "It's a bear!" I screamed imme-diately, burrowing deeper into my bag and covering my head. If it was a bear, I read somewhere it's a good idea to play dead, so that was going to be my strategy. Once again, I forgot that every bear in this part of the world was sound asleep in its den, and would remain so for a few more months. I also considered that it might be someone about to rob or hurt me, or worse. But I also wondered if maybe it was someone trying to save me, so I thought it might be worth a peak.

I slowly and cautiously stuck my head outside to look around and discovered that a huge pile of snow had fallen on top of me, apparently blown by the wind. After that there was no chance I would fall asleep, so I lay shivering, counting the minutes until dawn when I could get moving again.

When I caught the first glimmers of light in the sky, I'd never felt more relieved—well, that is, until I was rescued two years later on Everest. I survived! I'm alive! I couldn't believe I had made it through the night. I wiggled out of my bag, which had become a crust of ice and snow, threw everything I could into it, reattached my crampons for the slippery slope, and headed down as fast as I could run. I was in such a hurry that I took some wrong turns. I ended up lost and so had to retrace my steps. A few times I got stuck in waist-deep snow and had to dig myself out. But I didn't care about any of those things; I was just so happy to be alive.

By the time I got back to my car, my only thought was to get back down the mountain as fast as I could, so you probably won't be surprised to learn I got stuck again. And also once again I was totally on my own. After all, who would be crazy enough to come up here in the winter?

Sure enough, I was rescued once again, this time by a couple who casually walked up to the car and asked if they could help. "Well, sure," I stammered, utterly dumbfounded that these ghosts kept appearing, "But what are you guys *doing* here?"

"Oh," they both laughed, "we just came up here to see how much snow there is. Quite a lot, we see." Then they just disappeared once again.

That night on Whitney I had faced three of my biggest terrors: the fear of being alone, fear of the dark, and fear of the cold. Oh yeah, one more biggie—fear of death. I always thought I couldn't handle those things even if I could deal with almost anything else. Now I was reborn. Even though I twice failed to reach the Whitney summit, I still felt I'd achieved an amazing victory just to survive, realizing I could rely on myself to get out of trouble if I needed to.

So, What's Next?

As good as I felt about my survival skills under pressure, I still felt some unfinished business getting to the top of the damn mountain one way or the other. I waited until the spring thaw and finally reached the summit a few months later. As soon as I got back down, I immediately called International Climbing, and this time when the guy answered the phone, I told him, "Okay, I climbed Whitney like you told me to. What's next?"

Rather than brushing me off, this time the guide could tell I was completely serious about my plans. "Okay, that's a start. Next you've got to take some mountaineering courses and learn proper technique."

"Yeah? Like what?" I was curious what he had in mind for me.

"You have to learn everything! Your life is at stake. And so are the other team members who accompany you. If you do something stupid, or make a thoughtless mistake, it isn't just your life you are putting in jeopardy, but also the lives of those who are roped to you. One false move and you can take everyone else down with you. We'll teach you proper technique, safety procedures, crevasse rescue. . . "

"Crevasse? What's a crevasse?" I interrupted.

"It's a very, very deep crack in a glacier that can appear to have no bottom. If you fall into one of those suckers, you could end up on the other side of the world."

I laughed, but he ignored the interruption and just continued. "Then there's route finding, glacier travel, rope and belay techniques, rappelling, cramponing, rock climbing, and self-arrest."

I kept saying, "Uh huh," after each one on the list, afraid to display my further ignorance. Self-arrest? It sounded like I was supposed to arrest myself for some crime. But I later learned that refers to using your ice ax to stop yourself from falling off the mountain when you lose control and start slipping down an icy slope.

"Oh, and one more thing," he added.

"Yeah?" I was feeling overwhelmed at this point and really didn't want to hear "one more thing." But I tried to be polite.

"If you do end up climbing an 8,000-meter peak—that's over 26,000 feet—you'll be expected to carry your own pack. On Mt. Rainier, that's about 65 pounds, on Denali in Alaska, much more --85 pounds. Is that clear?"

"Sure," I answered, not at all sure. "But I only weigh 110 pounds."

"Then you'd better gain some weight and train more."

"But is it possible for someone my size to do this?"

He ignored the question and I wasn't sure what that meant, but just the prospect of doubt motivated me even more. I dramatically increased my training regimen, hiring a personal trainer who specialized in preparing mountaineers for summit attempts. I signed up for a series of courses as suggested, and then began progressively attacking more challenging climbs. I went with a team into the Cascade Mountains in Washington State, mostly to practice survival skills and to get used to functioning at high altitude. This was also the first time I was required to wear plastic mountaineering boots, big, heavy, sturdy footwear that provided the insulation and support I needed. After the first day, I counted 12 blisters on my left foot and 11 on my right.

Even with the suffering and annoyances operating in such difficult conditions, I was feeling really proud of my new skillset. I was getting good at tying knots, feeling strong on the climbs, and found that I had little trouble keeping up with the other team members, most of them men much, much bigger and stronger than I am. After completing the weeklong program, I again called International Climbing; by now the staff knew my story and we were on a first-name basis. I told them I finished the course. "So, *now* what's next? When do I get to climb Everest?"

"Hold on, there!" I was told. "You've still got a long way to go."

CHAPTER 6

⚸

Sara: Adventures in the Andes

January, 2014

I'D BEEN MAKING steady progress during the previous months, tackling progressively more difficult peaks to summit in the Western United States, but none of them were really close to the kinds of challenges I would face in the Himalayas. I needed to find some places where I could test myself at higher altitudes and that meant heading south toward the Andes.

It had been recommended to me by the guides that an excellent place for me to increase my training and strength would be to try the huge 6,000 meter volcanoes in Ecuador. All along the Pan-American Highway that crosses through the country are picture-perfect snow-capped peaks that rise up through the clouds. Since Ecuador is so-named because it straddles the equator, it is possible to climb really high mountains in relatively mild weather. And after my freezing night spent on top of Whitney, I still felt an aversion to the cold, one I would eventually have to overcome.

Matt wanted to come with me on the trip south, as much to learn more about what I was doing as to provide moral support. We had mapped out together the three main volcanoes I would attempt, beginning with Antisana (18,000 feet) and Cotopaxi (19,000 feet), before moving on to Chimborazo, which is the biggest of them all at 20,000 feet. All my ambition and excitement was immediately tempered when we first landed in Quito (9,300 feet) and I already had a headache and symptoms of altitude sickness.

I'm not sure what I was thinking when I considered the possibility of breaking my altitude record three times in 17 days by climbing each of these volcanoes with only a day or two rest between each expedition.

Although by Himalayan standards, the mountains are not especially frigid, the high winds, freezing rain, and constant snow can make the experience fairly miserable, as I was soon to learn. It probably didn't help that I had decided to share my plans to climb Everest with my team and guide who were, let us say, less than enthusiastic.

"Are you fucking *loca*, Sarita?" my guide said as he shook his head in bewilderment. He just looked at me and assumed a small woman couldn't possibly be strong enough to attempt something that he could never do.

Once the guide started in on me, it was open season among the other members of my climbing team. "Do you have some kind of death wish?" another woman kept asking me. One guy, perhaps also threatened by the possibility that I could do things beyond his capability, also kept badgering me every time I faltered. "See," he'd say to try to shame me, "how can you possibly *think* about doing Everest?" To be fair, however, there were also a few others on the team who quietly tried to encourage and support me, one of whom was a guy close to 80 years old who had run over 100 marathons.

I tried my best just to ignore them, but the criticisms were taking their toll on my (naïve?) confidence. Although I was feeling some discouragement and frustration with my progress, it was wonderful to spend time with Matt in this beautiful country. If during the days I was "working" in brutal conditions, it really helped that at night we could enjoy the amazing food and nightlife (when I could stay awake past 9 o'clock).

Too Humiliating to Quit

The idea behind our structured itinerary was to climb progressively higher mountains, resting and recovering in between each expedition. The final climb up Chimborazo would be brutal, not only because we'd be walking all night with no sleep, but because of the rarified air and hurricane-like winds.

Our first climb had the easiest approach imaginable: we took a gondola from the middle of Quito up to the top of a 12,000-foot volcano as our starting point. We were in full gear with our packs, helmets, heavy mountaineering boots, and all our equipment, which was kind of amusing since we'd seen all kinds of Ecuadorian families up there enjoying picnics and strolling around like it's a park (which it is). Here I was tromping around in my boots with trekking poles and I saw ladies strolling in heels or sandals, carrying their purses instead of backpacks.

The good news was that I ended up making the summit to 15,400 feet without much difficulty. I was really stoked because I'd never been that high before. My headache and slight nausea were totally manageable and I was feeling pretty strong.

Next on our menu was this gorgeous mountain called Antisana, which has a saddle on top leading to two different summits. The scenery was like a dream, with a glacial lake below us, wild horses running along the pastures, and views of the whole Quito valley. To add to the excitement, our team consisted of the only people anywhere around.

We had been practicing our roping and self-arrest techniques. This is what you are supposed to do if there is some disaster and you have the misfortune to slip and start sliding into a crevasse or over a cliff. You are supposed to flip over onto your belly and simultaneously dig in with the tips of your crampons and ice ax. In theory this is designed to stop you from careening down the slippery slope. In practice, however, when you are roped up with three other people, it might not work that well if the person in front of you starts falling and drags the rest of the team down with her.

I got the first inkling of possible trouble when a substitute guide showed up to lead us who appeared to me to be somewhat complacent and less than highly motivated. He kept saying, "Take it easy," *tranquilo*, and *despacio*. "Take it slowly." That's fine, but what we all needed was a push, not permission to chill out.

For any big climb, the strategy is usually to leave some time before midnight, when the glacier is frozen solid and avalanches would be minimal. During the day, once the sun heats up the ice and snow, the danger increases exponentially—plus there is the added grind of moving in slushy, heavy snow in which you sink to your knees or mid-thighs with every step. The plan is to get to the summit before first light, enjoy the view for a few minutes as the sun rises, and then race down (which takes only a few hours) before the mountain becomes unstable.

For reasons I didn't understand, our guide kept us at a low altitude for our base camp. That meant we would have to climb more than 5,000 feet during the night. In addition, rather than getting us going at the usual time, we left four hours late. By the time we'd been going for a few hours, I was already feeling sick. I was so tired from lack of sleep that I could barely keep my eyes open; I was just shuffling along on autopilot trying not to vomit and to keep my head from exploding.

I realized that I hadn't fueled myself properly and didn't have enough nutrition in my system. Getting up this high, beyond 17,000 feet, I also didn't realize how hard it would be to catch my breath. My heart was pounding so hard in my chest that it scared me. I was certain I wasn't getting enough oxygen, and that's when all the cramps began. It was obvious to me at this point that I was not nearly prepared and strong enough to climb such a high summit that was still only a baby peak compared to what I had in mind. It seemed that everyone who had been warning and discouraging me had been right, and I was ready to just turn around and call this whole thing off.

That's when the winds started to pick up. It felt like it was going to blow me right off the edge of the mountain. There were times I had to just stop, dig in my pole, turn my back to the wind, and just hold on until I could take another step. Once we arrived at a vertical ice wall, we were temporarily sheltered from the wind: that's the good news; the bad news was that now I had to climb the damn thing and I was already breathing pretty heavily and sweating through my clothes, freezing the condensation to my body. I noticed that, surprisingly, I still wasn't hungry or thirsty, which might have been a good thing because my water bottles were now frozen solid.

The night was completely dark. The only illumination possible was from my headlamp, as well as those from other team members. I decided that was a gift of sorts because the one time I decided to peer over the edge of the ridge we were climbing, there was a deep crevasse that didn't seem to end. Better that I just kept my light and eyes right in front of me. I was becoming so terrified of falling that I forgot how hard I was breathing. I started to climb the wall just as fast as I could, hoping to get to safety as soon as possible and enjoy some rest. The few times I stopped to eat, the energy bars were frozen solid. I thought I'd break my teeth.

There was this constant dialogue going on inside my head where I kept negotiating with myself. "In five more minutes, if I don't feel any better, I'll take a break." "If this headache doesn't go away in the next half hour, I'll turn back." And then, being mathematically inclined, I tried to estimate what percentage of energy I thought I might have left. I came up with a rather precise answer of "seven percent," which didn't inspire much confidence. Since I was roped to my partners, before I could change my mind, I would just get pulled along. Given what I told the others about my plans, it felt too humiliating to quit.

I Lost My Motivation—and a Part of Myself

Climbing a big mountain is a grind. There's usually nothing to see because it is dark during the ascent. It's just one endless footstep after another, following the snaking headlights ahead, one step, two steps, four steps, breathe, rest. Repeat. Over and over and over again. After hours of this grueling routine, I could see the first glimmer of the sun about to peak over the far ridge. There was this incredible golden line across the horizon and, for the first time, I could actually see all the spectacular volcanoes and valleys around us. Even though I still had a headache and nausea, I was temporarily distracted enough to notice this was the most beautiful thing I'd ever seen, (almost) making it worth all the suffering and aggravation.

This joy didn't last more than a minute before I realized what bad shape I was in. Not only was I absolutely exhausted, but I felt totally disoriented, barely aware of where I was and what I was doing there. I kept collapsing to the ground, then wondering how I got there. I'd slowly, agonizingly, use my trekking pole in one hand and my ice ax in the other, to pull myself back to a standing position. Then I'd take another step or two and end up on the ground again. It felt hopeless and I wondered how I could possibly continue. At this point I was also wondering how I was going to get back down, no longer concerned with reaching the summit.

In my fog I heard one of the other team members announce that he'd had enough and was going back down. Before I could think about whether I wanted to join him or not, the rest of the climbers attached to his rope immediately decided to join mine, which I was none too happy about. I had enough problems already without having to deal with another group of climbers who would likely climb at a different rhythm and pace. This one guy, in particular, kept pulling on my rope to make me go faster so I just pulled back. Finally, I was so angry and frustrated with him I started screaming at him, "Goddamn it! Will you stop pulling on the damn rope and leave me alone!" I heard the words coming out of my mouth, but it was as if they belonged to someone else. I no longer recognized myself.

Only later would I realize that I was experiencing the most severe form of altitude symptoms, high altitude cerebral edema. I knew that *something* was wrong with me, but I wasn't thinking clearly enough to know what was happening. Because of increasing fluid accumulation in my tissue, the symptoms would never dissipate until I headed back down to a much lower altitude. I was especially worried because I'd eaten so little food, had no appetite, and all I could think about was trying to avoid throwing up.

"Just get it over with," one of the guides instructed me. "Just throw up and you'll feel better."

Easy for him to say. I was barely keeping myself together. I was wondering how I could possibly continue when the lead guide announced we couldn't make the summit that morning because the ice bridge had collapsed. I could hear some token grumbling, but I think all of us were relieved that we could head back down to safety and warmth. And once we descended a few thousand feet rather quickly, I could already feel myself recovering. As dispirited as I now felt, I glanced over my shoulder and could see Cotopaxi in the distance, with its symmetrical ice cream-topped snowcap glistening in the sun. I knew that was where we were headed in a few more days.

I lost something of myself that night. I lost my motivation to do this climbing. This was just a miserable experience quite different than the day hikes I'd been doing back home. I was sore and tired and decided I'd had enough. I thought I might feel better after I had a decent meal and caught up on some sleep. That wasn't exactly the case, especially after I felt further discouraged when one of the guides remarked that there were just some people who couldn't handle high altitude. He was implying that I was one of those people.

Round Two

LIKE A PUNCH drunk boxer still reeling from too many hits to the head, I wasn't quite myself when we began the ascent of Cotopaxi a few days later. As usual, it was windy and sleeting. After just two hours on the trail I already looked like a human icicle. Once again I had a splitting headache, no appetite, but I soldiered on, determined that this time I was going to reach the top even if it killed me.

I climbed in a stupor all night long, eight solid hours of walking in the dark. Once again I kept my eyes and my headlamp focused only on my feet and the space ahead of me. Some of the time we were walking on a knife edge of a ridge and a fall would surely mean death as I couldn't imagine that anything would save me. At times the glacier was so steep that we had to sidestep up the slope. At other times, it was once again just a long, endless, brutal slog. Remarkably, somehow we were now approaching the summit that was just 50 meters away—the top was literally within a snowball's throw.

I saw a guy coming down from the top. He was so covered in snow and ice that at first he didn't look human at all. His eyelashes and beard were frozen solid. "How was the view?" I called out to him.

"What view?" he answered through the howling wind. "It's like being in a hurricane up there. It's hard to even stay upright without getting blown off."

That's all I needed to hear. What was the point of getting to the top if the only reason is to say you did it? There was no view, no enjoyment of the moment, just bitter, bitter cold that drives you into the ground.

That was it. I'd now had quite enough of this business. Once again I wouldn't make it to the summit even if we got close. I know Jeffrey has his own story to tell about this climb because he later followed my footsteps to this place. I should have warned him more about how terrible my experience really was. It's kind of like the way some mothers describe childbirth—once it's over they say it was the best experience of their lives, even though, during the time, it is excruciatingly agonizing.

My legs felt rubbery and insubstantial. Most people think that getting to the summit is the hardest part about a climb and I suppose it is in the sense that it is the most physically demanding part. But it's usually on the way down that most people get injured or die because of their exhaustion and sense of urgency. You aren't thinking straight. You are likely descending too fast. Once again I kept falling until, at one point, disaster occurred when I fell right into a deep crevasse. I found myself hanging from a rope as I heard people screaming, but strangely, I wasn't scared. On the contrary, I was fascinated by the eerie deep turquoise color of the cave, with huge icicles hanging down from every surface: It was so beautiful I thought for a moment that I had died.

Then I felt myself being hauled out of the hole with everyone on the team working in unison, absolutely freaked out by my close call. The guide was angry at me because I forgot to yell "Falling!" as I sailed off the edge. There were a few other things I considered yelling as I lost my balance, but "Falling!" wasn't one of them. Anyway, I was certainly grateful for the rescue so that I might live and climb another day.

Round Three. . . Postponed

It took me three days to mostly recover from the previous failed climb and there was still one more to go, the highest of them all, Chimborazo. This volcano is actually 7,000 feet higher than the top of Everest—at least if you measure from the center of the earth. It would also be a much tougher climb than anything I had yet attempted, which made me feel even more ambivalent about this whole thing.

Just before I started preparing my equipment for the climb, I decided to check my email one last time because I'd been waiting to hear about a teaching position in computer science at a university in southern California (where I would soon meet Jeffrey and learn about the foundation he had started). This was the dream job that I had worked all my life to attain, and I was over the moon excited about this opportunity. I also realized that with the commitment of teaching full semesters, I would no longer have the time to devote to my training. Maybe this was the excuse I was looking for to cancel, or at least postpone, my plan? In any case, I decided there was no longer any compelling reason to subject myself to more suffering on this trip: I had already learned that this mountain climbing business was perhaps too difficult to pursue. It never really made much sense to me that people would spend all that time and money, and actually risk their lives, just to get to the top of a mountain. Maybe it's a male thing or something, but this just never resonated with me; I needed some other motive or reason to do this that wasn't just about my own personal glory, but for some larger purpose. And I had no idea yet what that might be.

At the last minute, I decided to cancel my final climb and rest at the hut at 16,000 feet until the rest of the group returned, but because of the bad weather the whole climb was cancelled. We went back to Quito for a couple of days before heading back home.

I was soon fully immersed in my new career as an electrical engineering and computer science professor, teaching at two different universities. This meant that as a new hire, I had to accept almost any class offered, regardless of the specific subject and time it was offered. Even if I had wanted to continue my training, I would no longer have time to do so. Sure, there was still some unfinished business to deal with, but for now it was the most exciting adventure of all for me to become a college instructor teaching the subjects I loved the most.

It was while completing my first semester teaching at California State University, Fullerton that someone suggested that I make contact with another professor on campus who also enjoyed climbing mountains and was doing a lot of work in Nepal. I immediately sent him a message, asking if we could meet to learn more about the things he was doing. It just seemed like a strange coincidence that this guy was spending so much time in the area where I yearned to go, but he wasn't doing so just to climb or trek, but to help young girls.

As soon as I entered his office, Jeffrey gave me the warmest, most inviting smile, as if we were already old friends. "So," he started the conversation, "what do you teach here? I haven't seen you before."

"That's because this is my first semester," I explained, still feeling a bit shy. My friends had told me that Dr. Kottler had written more books than most people ever read and he was an international scholar. "Anyway, I teach courses in data structure and micro-electronics."

"I have no idea what those are," he said with a grin, "but I'm glad somebody knows how to teach those things."

I asked him about Nepal and his experiences there, and rather than talking about his experiences in the Himalayas, he talked about the plight of girls there. He told me the story of how he got started there many years ago when he was working on a research project and the ways that women and girls were treated in that country, sometimes forced into slavery.

Everything I knew about Nepal was related to climbing Everest because I had been single-minded in my focus. I had yet to consider what life was like there for the people who live in remote areas. Jeffrey explained how difficult and challenging life was for girls from the lowest caste, and that more than 10,000 Nepali girls were smuggled across the border into India every year.

It seemed like during this conversation, and a few others that followed, everything changed for me in my mission. I felt like I had to do something to help these children, and I started wondering if there was a way I could combine my initial goal with somehow bringing greater public awareness to the plight of the girls. Sometimes I can be rather impulsive (as you may have noticed). I surprised myself when I announced out loud to Jeffrey that I intended to climb Everest to plant the flag of Empower

Nepali Girls on the highest spot in the world. But more than that, I vowed that I would raise at least $29,000 for the girls, one dollar for every foot of the mountain.

It's strange to me how that realization was so transformative for me. As I mentioned, it never made much sense to me to put up with all the hard work and pain just to climb a mountain—unless there was some larger purpose. I wasn't willing to risk my life for some stupid bragging rights, but it made complete sense to me to do so for others who couldn't advocate on their own behalf.

As soon as I left Jeffrey's office, I began forming a new plan. There had to be some way I could continue my teaching responsibilities and yet also renew my commitment to training harder than ever before. In the past all I'd done was fail at most every big mountain I tried to climb, but now I felt a new sense of purpose. I hadn't yet met any of the girls but I already loved them just from Jeffrey's stories and the photos and videos I watched on the Empower Nepali Girls website. Given where I came from, and what I had to live through as a girl in Iran, I felt a deep connection to these girls. I saw a part of myself in every one of them. And I thought by saving them I would find a greater purpose.

A New Plan

My mind was racing with ideas and possibilities for raising money to support my Everest fundraising idea (In my mind it was no longer about the climb but about how I could inspire and support the girls through my actions). It occurred to me that when I was having moments of doubt during climbs, when I felt exhausted and wanted to give up, the girls would inspire me to keep going—not for myself, but for them.

Of course I'd never tried fundraising before, but that didn't stop me. I'd also never been climbing before I decided to scale Everest. The Persian community in Southern California is very tight-knit and also quite generous in helping less fortunate people. Although I did get some questions from some within the community as to why I wasn't helping Persian girls instead of the Hindu/Buddhist children in a country they'd barely heard of, I explained that it didn't matter who we were helping as long as we were doing *something* to make the world a better place.

I tried all kinds of things to get started, organizing dinner parties, silent auctions, lectures, charity events, using social media to publicize my plans and asking for support. I was shocked not only by how many friends and family joined my effort, but also that I had a talent for this kind of thing. Even though I was still a neophyte, I loved that I could measure my success by the amount of money flowing in to support the girls. Now it was time to get back into training if I was still serious about doing this.

"Hello," I reintroduced myself to the people at International Climbing, who hadn't heard from me in a while and must have assumed I had disappeared. "It's me again, the lady who wants to climb Everest but hadn't had any mountaineering experience."

"Yes?" the guide said on the other end of the phone. I don't really think he had any idea who I was so I reviewed for him what I'd been told earlier. "I took the advice and tried climbing Whitney, then Rainier, then I went to Ecuador and did the volcanoes there as you told me to do."

"Yeah? How did it go?"

"Fine," I lied. "So, tell me. What's next?"

The guide explained that now that I'd completed all those preliminary training climbs, I needed to demonstrate that I could handle a 7,000-meter peak before I could join one of their expeditions.

"Okay, then, where should I go?"

"You say you've done Ecuador?"

I'm not sure what he meant by "done," but I had certainly spent time on some of those volcanoes.

"The next mountain you should try, then, is Aconcagua," he mentioned with only a moment's thought.

"Oh yeah? Where's that?" I asked him.

"It's in Argentina, near the Chilean border. It's the highest mountain in the Western Hemisphere, over 23,000 feet high. Let us know when you've done that and then we can talk about you joining one of our quali-fying expeditions in the Himalayas."

This wasn't going to be like Ecuador at all where I could go up and down in two days. This climb was going to take close to a month, with 20 days spent continuously on the glacier. I planned to do a few things dif-ferently, starting with upping my training regimen. I also decided I wasn't going to tell anyone on the trip about my Everest plans because I was tired of people making fun of me. Best to just keep that to myself.

I had already been exposed to high winds on the Ecuadorian vol-canoes, but I wasn't prepared for the hurricane force I encountered on Aconcagua. It wasn't supposed to be that technical of a climb, but when you are trying to sleep in a tent at high altitude with 60 mile-per-hour winds threatening to blow you off the mountain, I had no choice but to slip back into survival mode like I remembered on that lonely night on Whitney. This time, however, at least I wasn't alone in my misery.

We had to spend two nights and three days trapped in our tents because it wasn't safe to venture outside. This was also the first time I learned the "funnel technique" for peeing in a bottle, an absolute neces-sity for women who don't have the same luxury of simply inserting an organ into the opening. All I could do during that time was try to stay as warm as possible in my sleeping bag and stare at the mesh ceiling of the tent since sleep was out of the question.

When the high winds finally diminished to only "raging," we geared up and began climbing again, this time to Camp IV at 21,000 feet, the highest point I'd ever reached. This would be our final staging area for the summit attempt after spending a few more days acclimatizing to the rari-fied air. Given that sleep was out of the question at such altitude, it wasn't exactly restful hanging out waiting for the weather to clear. Everything is challenging at that altitude: it takes forever just to boil water and prepare a meal. And one of the biggest challenges is consuming enough calories to maintain strength after so many days on the mountain. We were all getting anxious and excited for the final stage.

First Taste of Salami

There was a mystery in our little camp that a few of us were trying to solve. We noticed a solitary abandoned tent on the edge of our ridge, one of the few reasonably flat spaces before the mountain rose in a steep, vertical wall. The tent was mostly tattered by the high winds, but when we investigated inside, we noticed there was some valuable gear inside. When we asked one of the guides why the tent was there and who it belonged to, he just shrugged and pointed to the summit. Apparently two climbers had left for the summit a few days earlier and were now trapped somewhere on the way up. We could see a helicopter flying over us, presumably to try and rescue them, but we later learned their bodies were never found.

As if that wasn't enough of a bad omen, there was another tent in the vicinity with two climbers who were so sick they couldn't move. Our guides intervened to pack them up and send them back down so that they might survive before they became worse. Watching these two incidents made us all even more concerned about our safety.

There is a problem for high climbers in that at high altitude, you burn something like 5,000 calories per day and it's virtually impossible to replace all that lost energy. In addition, you usually have no appetite in general, which is compounded by the tasteless freeze-dried food and energy bars. Our guides kept reminding us to eat and drink as much as we could, even though it was just one more chore we had to get done.

If consuming enough food and water was one difficulty, then another was dealing with things on the other end, so to speak. Constipation was killing me as we kept going higher and higher. In order to have a bowel movement, I had to either use the vestibule of my tent where the flap folds over, which is fairly disgusting, or else I had to wander out on the glacier in the freezing wind, in full view of everyone else since there was nothing to hide behind. I had never considered how hard it was to do anything up here and how many of my prior "rules" as a modest Persian woman I would have to break.

Growing up in a Muslim country, I had never tasted pork in my life. We had been told all our lives that eating the meat of a pig was an instant ticket to Hell. So I was taken aback when one of our guides thrust his hand inside my tent with some kind of meat.

"What is that?" I asked him. Frankly, I didn't really care as I was starving for some kind of protein other than the energy bars.

"Salami," he said, as if that was obvious.

I wasn't sure what salami was exactly. "Is it beef?" I asked him.

He shook his head and said the forbidden word. "Pork."

There were fireworks going off in my muddled brain. On the one hand it seemed like this was a temptation from the devil, testing me, but I've never been very religious—and besides, I was starving. So I carefully put a small piece of the meat in my mouth and found it to be the single most delicious meal I've ever had. I had never tasted salami or pork before and now I wondered how I could have possibly missed such an amazing treat. Even today, whenever I see or smell salami somewhere, I immediately think about our camp on Aconcagua. And if I made it to the top or not, if I survived or not, I reassured myself at least I got to taste salami!

The First Persian Woman

As hard as I was trying to keep my morale up and pacifying my fears after learning about the deaths that occurred just above us, my tent-mate was making things worse. She was really discouraged and told me she was giving up. Rather than respecting and honoring her choice, in some ways a courageous one given how far she'd come already, I tried to talk her into changing her mind. It felt like if she gave up, then it would be easier for me to do the same. And this time, I desperately wanted to prove I could bag a peak. In spite of my attempts to convince her, I finally recognized that she was so weak, she was going to have enough difficulty just getting down the mountain in one piece.

The days wore on, with very little change in routines. It was like we were hibernating, waiting for a break in the weather. And then, finally, it was summit night and we tried to grab a few hours of sleep, or at least rest. For some reason I actually had an appetite and was able to down a huge breakfast—dehydrated eggs, dehydrated potatoes, and of course, salami!

I packed and prepared all my equipment, gave my tent-mate a big hug, and told her I'd get to the top for both of us. She just gave me a sick smile and buried herself back in her sleeping bag. She was crying and barely holding herself together.

It was so, so, so cold outside, but once we started climbing, I immediately felt warm. And strong! As we ascended slowly, steadily, it felt like my hands were burning up. I didn't realize at the time that this is one of the crazy symptoms of high altitude. Some climbers have been known to rip off all their clothes in the delusion that they are burning up when they are actually freezing to death.

One of the guides saw me take my gloves off and immediately walked over to me, knowing what was happening. At this point I was actually in serious danger of getting frostbite as I could no longer feel any sensation in my fingers. "I have to go back down! Right away!" I told him. I'm an engineer. I can't possibly lose my fingers or I'm out of business.

The guide started arguing with me, absolutely insistent that we could continue. Meanwhile, he was rubbing my hands between his own, trying to get some sensation back into them, eventually succeeding. He put my gloves back on and then added a pair of over-mittens to further insulate me. The dude saved my hands!

We continued up, up, up, up. Every so often I could hear the lead guide call out, "One hour to the top," trying to encourage us. Then, "Thirty minutes to the summit." Then, "Twenty minutes." We were getting closer and closer with every step, and this time I just knew I was going to make it. And then, suddenly it seemed, I was standing on top of the highest point in all of the Western and Southern Hemispheres. I could look around and see the whole world spread out before me.

Enjoying the view from Aconcagua in the Andes, the highest mountain outside of Asia at close to 23,000 feet. Although not a very technical climb, this was my first success reaching a major summit.

Nobody was more surprised than I was that I had made it to the top. Given my past failures, I just assumed I didn't have the stamina or the kind of body that could tolerate high altitudes. Given that I spent my whole life at sea level, that isn't a far stretch. But now that I had reached the summit, it felt like I had just fallen in love. I was incredibly happy. I started screaming into the wind, "I made it! I made it!"

I thought about the price I had paid for this joy. I was so exhausted and cold that I could barely remain upright. My face was swollen and sunburned. I'd lost all the weight that I had worked so hard to gain. After four months of diligent training, four months of abstaining from alcohol and other indulgences, all I could think about was getting back down the mountain and sampling some of the amazing Argentinian wines.

We all celebrated together once we arrived at the bottom. As exhausted as I felt, I was proud of what I'd accomplished: I was the first

Persian woman to summit Aconcagua. To add to my excitement, I had confided earlier to our lead guide that I intended to climb Everest, and although, at first, he kind of rolled his eyes, now he looked at me differently. "Have you ever heard of Aida?" he asked me.

"Aida?"

"*Si, ella es la primera mujer*—Yes, she is the first woman—from Saudi Arabia to climb Everest."

I wondered why he was telling me this. I steeled myself, expecting another round of scolding, when he really surprised me. "But, Sara, you are stronger than Aida. You actually did quite well on the mountain. Although you were tired, you had a lot of energy on the way down. And this whole time you took care of your tent-mate when she was having trouble, and did so without complaint."

I was speechless and didn't quite know how to respond to that.

"Every time I looked back," he continued, "I saw you following me closely. You still have a lot of work left to do, but I think you will do it. *Tienes fuerte*. You are strong. You have, how you say, *buena tecnica*, good technique for someone so new to the sport. I think you are ready for what comes next, whatever that might be."

That was the very first time a professional climber encouraged me. That meant so much. Plus, now I was doing this for something so much bigger than myself.

CHAPTER 7

— ❧ —

Jeffrey: I Followed Sara's Footsteps

May, 2014

AFTER HEARING ABOUT some of Sara's adventures, with the worst parts initially left out, I found myself yearning to create some of my own. As a psychotherapist for so many years, I've learned over time that the stories people tell about their experiences do not necessarily reflect what really happened. We tend to gloss over the hard parts and instead revel in the triumphs and glories. Whether talking about climbing a mountain, or any other transformative event, most people tend to "forget" the misery and suffering involved, and instead remember only the best parts. Still, it sounded like Sara was having so much fun and learning so much about herself with this new hobby of hers that I wanted some of the action as well. Sara talked a lot about how I've influenced her through work with the girls, but she has had just as much of an impact on me.

The main challenge I have in trying to keep up with Sara, or at least follow in her footsteps, is the 30-year difference in our ages. Lately I'd been struggling with adjusting to the symptoms of aging, and found that things that I used to be able to do were now so much more difficult. I had always thought that aging was a relatively gradual, incremental process that proceeded in an orderly fashion from one stage to the next. I've taught courses in human development over the years, so I'm more than a little familiar with all the theories and research on the subject. So, I was quite dumbfounded to discover that within a ridiculously short period of time, I became old. My body was indeed slowing down and my mind was not what it used to be.

I have come to accept that there are some things I can't do any more. I just don't have the energy or the motivation to work that hard anymore. I've lost some ambition. I feel much more selective and discriminating about how I want to spend my time. I feel the clock ticking down and realize that if there are still some things I want to do, I had better get going. I no longer take for granted that I will necessarily be around all that much longer.

I've had more than my fair share of adventures in my lifetime, living in a half dozen different countries, climbing mountains in Greenland, Iceland, Nepal, Peru, and other places around the globe. I've even done a little bit of technical climbing on Mt. Rainier and some trekking peaks in the Himalayas, but I figured if I wanted to summit a really big, challenging mountain, I'd better do it soon. After hearing about Sara's "wonderful" adventures in Ecuador (She forgot to tell me about the wind and cold), I took it upon myself to prepare for climbing some 19,000-foot volcanoes. Sara thought this was a fabulous idea. She encouraged me to pursue this goal, just as she was following her own dream.

I started training for the expedition with ferocious commitment, increasing my workout regimens several hours each day. I "invested" in mountaineering equipment and trained to become comfortable with my boots, crampons, and other stuff. I spent hours on a stair climber with a backpack full of books on my back. I planned my acclimatization to high altitude with careful and meticulous incremental adjustments. After all, I wasn't a young man anymore, and I wanted to survive this experience more than I needed to summit the volcanoes.

Things did not quite go according to my plan in that my guide turned out to be more interested in getting me to the top than being worried about my safety. For some reason he felt competitive with me. He seemed to take pleasure out of shaming and cajoling me to go faster and harder. I had been spoiled all my years in the Himalayas where the Sherpas are so supportive and helpful, practically carrying someone up the mountain if that is what is needed. All I'd usually hear from my guide, Enrico, was, *"Nos vamos."* "Let's go." or *"Apurate!"* "Hurry up!"

We began the summit of Cotopaxi at 10 PM, having to start several hours earlier than usual because of closed facilities at the preferred staging point which was at a higher altitude. As we climbed up, up, up, I tried to get into a rhythm that felt comfortable, a task that was becoming increasingly challenging as we ascended higher. I could feel Enrico pulling me on the rope, urging me to go faster. I wasn't sure why it was so important that we move so quickly, instead of at my own pace, but maybe it was because we had to start so much further down the mountain and needed to make up time before the snow softened.

It was completely dark, our trail lit by headlamps directed only at the next few steps ahead. Sara had told me that the glacier was speckled with deep crevasses, but I was still surprised when I looked to the left or right and saw we were walking on the knife-edge of a ridge with a drop-off of thousands of feet on each side. I kept trying to rehearse in my mind what to do if I slipped. For some strange reason all I could think of that was that it was important to yell, "Falling!" like Sara forgot to do when she slipped into the crevasse. I was tired of Enrico yelling at me. Oh, did I mention I'm afraid of heights?

My breathing was becoming ragged and I started feeling light-headed as we topped over 18,000 feet. It had been a long, long night so far climbing for five hours. And just like Sara's climb, it was the usual weather on Cotopaxi—rain, sleet, snow, and 50-mile-an-hour winds. I kept asking myself every few minutes, "*Why* did I think this was a good idea?"

It was about three o'clock in the morning, still hours from the summit, when I kept hearing this voice inside my head becoming more and more strident. "You know, you don't have to do this. You can stop any time you want." It felt like I was hallucinating because the voice seemed to come from someone else. I looked ahead at Enrico trudging along at his own comfortable pace and wondered for a moment whether he was the one speaking to me. But he ignored me most of the time. I was just a burden to him, a package to deliver to the top.

I could barely catch my breath anymore. I'd take two steps, then need to rest for a moment, leaning on my pole before I could feel Enrico yanking my rope once again. *"Nos vamos!* Let's go!" he'd say with an infuriating smile, almost seeming to enjoy my discomfort and difficulty. This time when he pulled on my rope, I yanked it back as hard as I could, almost pulling him over. I could hear him swearing at me, and I stifled a giggle of satisfaction.

A happy climber before trying to summit Cotopaxi volcano in the distance.

It was in that moment that I realized that I was in *way* over my ability. I was too old, or at least too old to climb at someone else's pace, someone who was much younger than me (and a professional mountaineer). I had to respect my limits—and my age. So I unhooked the rope from my waist, turned off my headlamp, and lay down on the glacier staring up at the moon. "I'm not going any further," I announced. "I don't have to do this anymore," giving voice to the mantra inside my head. "I just want to sit here and enjoy where I am. I want to look at the moon. I want to listen to the glacier. I earned this."

I stripped off my pack, stuck my ax into the ice, and just lay down on the glacier. The skies had temporarily cleared for a few minutes before the next blizzard would begin, so I could see the whole universe above me. I could hear the sounds of the glacier groaning as it settled and resettled itself, an animal-like sound, as if it was truly alive. I could almost feel it pulsing underneath me.

I lay there for I don't know how long. It could have been ten minutes or a half-hour, I'm not sure. I tried to just ignore Enrico, who was sitting off by himself eating a snack and humming to himself. At least he was leaving me alone for a change.

In some ways, those few peaceful minutes on the glacier, just lying there and listening to the glacial movements, made the whole trip worthwhile. During this interlude, there was no suffering or discomfort, just complete and utter peace. I never wanted the experience to end—except that I was now getting quite cold and it was time to complete the descent.

Enrico didn't seem to care if we stayed there or not, but I could see he was becoming increasingly restless to keep going. All I wanted to do was get down the mountain and feel warm again. I was surrendering to the realities of my age. It was time to accept my limitations and make do with what was still within my capability. I learned a hard lesson, but perhaps one that would serve me well during this next stage of life. It seemed my mountaineering days were over.

The Power of Stories

I've long had an interest in the power of storytelling to promote transformation and long-lasting changes, whether in the context of teaching, therapy, or in books such as this. Perhaps you've already been hooked on a story we've already told that penetrates you, sticks with you, reminds you of something similar in your own life, or perhaps even inspires you in some way. In my research I've learned that the brain has evolved as essentially a "storied organ," one that automatically converts all experiences into relatively coherent narratives. Dreams are essentially memory fragments caused by randomly-firing neurons during sleep, but they appear to us as stories that may be bizarre at times and seem to make little sense, but that is just our brain doing its job. It turns out that stories we hear and read and view are often as real to our brains as anything we might actually experience in our daily lives. That's one reason why telling a story to someone can sometimes provoke new insights and understandings that perhaps couldn't happen any other way.

When I returned from Ecuador, in some ways I was actually proud of my decision to *not* reach the summit. I thought this was quite an excellent example of wise and mature decision making. I even went so far as to imagine that I was truly advanced enough in my development that I could accept gracefully the things I couldn't do anymore. And this was the story that I told to a group of students after I returned, featuring the lesson learned about myself and what it could mean.

It was about a week later that one of the students in the class sent me a message about something she wanted me to know. Apparently that very weekend after our class, she and her husband went for a hike in the desert. After about an hour on the trail, mostly climbing up to a ridge with a viewpoint, she found she couldn't go any further and stopped to rest. Her husband was urging her to continue but she kept shaking her head, needing to rest.

"I just couldn't walk anymore," she said. "I felt dizzy and light-headed from the heat. I was just so disappointed in myself and quite frustrated. It felt like I had failed myself."

The woman told me she started crying, then sobbing inconsolably, in spite of her husband's attempts to calm her down. "But then, suddenly, your story popped into my head. I remember you lying down on the ice and looking up at the stars and noticing how beautiful the place was, even though you were so tired."

The story seemed to sneak up on her, kind of hanging in her brain, waiting for the right moment to provide some personal revelation. "I realized that there was no reason we absolutely had to get to the top of the ridge. The scenery was plenty gorgeous where we already were. So I forced myself to look around and appreciate where I was with all these endless miles of desert all around us in every direction. I wiped away my tears and hugged my husband because we were sharing this together. Then, we slowly walked back down hand-in-hand."

The woman ended the message by relating how it was my story of quitting, of failure, of giving myself permission to enjoy where I was, instead of somewhere else I thought I needed to be, that gave her comfort and reassurance. I felt so proud of both of us.

Alas, Not the End of the Story

If this sounds like a happy ending, that I accepted my limitations of aging, then I'm not being totally forthcoming. After I returned and told Sara about my misfortune on Cotopaxi, she confessed to me that she hadn't made it to the summit either. It's not that she had been hiding anything from me; I just didn't think to ask her much about the climb itself other than what equipment I'd need.

But once I learned that Sara hadn't made it to the top, it felt like I still had unfinished business on that mountain. I guess some lessons just don't stick. I figured if I prepared differently, trained harder, and especially worked with a different guide, I could conquer that sucker after all. I also planned to bring my wife, Ellen, with me for moral support.

When I contacted the mountaineering company in Ecuador, they promised me I could have a different guide, and even offered me a repeat customer discount. I was waiting outside the *hosteria* where I was staying for my pick-up when who shows up but Enrico! This is impossible I thought, since I'd especially requested *any* other guide except him.

It turned out that whereas he didn't remember anything about me on the climb, he did recall I was a big tipper. I guess I have a soft heart, and I'd learned long ago that giving generous gifts can sometimes change someone's life. Even though he was a total jerk, I had still rewarded him generously and he had somehow maneuvered the schedule so that he was the only guide available. To make matters worse, I was saddled with a German couple as part of my group who I'd already learned were the slowest walkers in the world. A few days earlier I'd done an acclimatizing hike with them and I ended up having to wait an hour for them in the car before we could return to our lodging. I, therefore, made certain that Enrico promised I'd have my own transportation back to the lodge when we finished the climb.

I had still been optimistic about my chances of summiting because I knew that the upper lodge was now open so we could begin the climb a few hours earlier than last time and start a few thousand feet higher, which would definitely help. Unfortunately, Enrico explained we'd be staying at the same place as last time because he'd forgotten to make a reservation at the high camp. Foiled again!

This time when we began the climb at 9 PM—three hours earlier than should have been necessary—I was feeling particularly strong. I had made sure to fuel up as much as I could, forcing food down my throat. I'd still not gotten any sleep during our rest time, but I could feel my adrenaline flowing with anticipation.

By the time we reached the high camp where everyone else was staying, it was close to midnight and they were all gearing up, seemingly well rested and well fed. Me? I was already tired. By the time we all left together, the German couple was still way behind.

Things went spectacularly well during the night. It was remarkably clear. In all the time I'd spent in Ecuador during these trips, I'd never actually had a clear night without a cloud in the sky. The only ominous news was that Cotopaxi, as an active volcano, was due for a major eruption. There were billows of steam flowing off the top.

There were at least a half-dozen other teams heading for the summit besides Enrico and me with only one very narrow trail of switchbacks across and over the glacier. We kept trying to pass the teams ahead of us. As I mentioned, Enrico was a fast walker, but this time I was keeping up with him. He also must have been in a better mood this time because he seemed unusually gracious and patient with me.

Of course, a few hours later, the freezing rain and sleet started to come down, blowing horizontally with the strong winds. Once we reached over 18,000 feet, things got even worse, with absolutely no visibility. Now I started wondering once again what the point was of reaching the top if there'd be no views. I talked with a climber on his way down and he discouraged me even further by saying it wasn't worth the bother to reach the summit since the steam from the volcano was pouring out and there was still a snowstorm.

I realized that my main goal—or at least this is what I told myself—was not so much to get to the top as to have some views of the neighboring countryside and all the other volcanoes along the horizon. It was approaching sunrise and I could see the orange glow along the horizon. Miraculously, the weather started to clear and the darkening sky of nighttime was actually turning fluorescent blue. This is what I'd wanted to see all along—the views!

One of the rare days when rain, fog, and clouds are
lifted to reveal Cotopaxi in all its glory.

Even though my legs were rubbery and my back was killing me, it was a wonderful trip down. I kept stopping to take photos of the ice caves and hoodoos (ice towers), as well as the incredible vistas of the valleys below us. It was magical, and Enrico was somewhat indulgent of my kid-like glee. Finally, I was having fun and it had nothing to do with getting to the top!

And Not the End of my Trails and Tribulations

Even with the frequent stops for photography, we managed to reach the bottom in just a few hours. I saw the German couple heading up as we were going down. They hadn't even made it halfway to the top yet while most of the others were already descending. I clarified with Enrico that I would not have to wait for them to go back to the *hosteria*. I was starving and cold and all I could think about was getting some sleep.

When we arrived back to the high camp Enrico decided to inform me that he had the only vehicle, and that we did, in fact, have to wait for the Germans. "You've got to be kidding me," I blurted out. "You promised I'd have my own transportation."

Enrico just shrugged in that typically Latino way that seemed to say, "No worries."

So, we waited. And waited. And waited. Did I mention we waited? For five damn hours! That's how much longer it took the German couple to get back down. Bless their hearts: they did get to the top and back, even though it took them something like 16 hours. I was so mad I could have spit. I had been shivering and starving. I was so sleep deprived I could barely think.

This mountaineering stuff: I'm glad that Sara has found her calling, but I've had enough.

CHAPTER 8

— ✤ —

Sara: Blowing in the Wind

July, 2014

AFTER MY EXPERIENCES climbing in South America, I was feeling much more confident. If I could survive on Aconcagua for almost three weeks, I realized that I was getting stronger and more resilient. For the first time I could actually imagine myself on Everest. I didn't know if I could make it to the top or not, but I was pretty sure I could give it a good try.

I'd come a very long way during the past two years, remembering my initial naive, feeble attempts. Not only had my strength and conditioning improved significantly, but I had learned much about climbing, weather, the mountains, even little tricks that experienced climbers take as second nature. Recently, Jeffrey and I went into the mountains together and I looked at his huge duffel filled with all the things he thought might be necessary and compared it to my own that was compressed to half the size. When climbing, reducing weight isn't just a luxury; it's absolutely critical.

Following my return from Aconcagua, Jeffrey had just come back from Nepal on one of his visits. He told me about a little girl who our foundation director, Pasang, found abandoned in a Buddhist temple in Kathmandu. This 5-year-old child, Nimsang, was lost and starving, so Pasang decided to bring her home and "adopt" her. Since then Pasang and his wife filled their home with other girls. The most recent one was an 8-year-old who had been sold to a family as a virtual slave. I eventually met this young girl, and I remember that while we were sitting at a table having a meal, I noticed that she would surround her plate with her arms as if afraid that someone would steal her food before she could put it in her mouth. I'm guessing that was how she was used to being treated.

When I heard about these children from Jeffrey, I felt helpless and heartbroken. It only renewed my commitment to do something really big in order to help them, even if it meant risking my own life. I felt more motivated than ever to complete this climb of Everest—but first I had some more training and preparation to do.

Ladders Over Nothingness

Mount Rainier in the Cascade Mountains of Washington is not particularly high (14,400 feet) or difficult to climb. Thousands of people do it every year, most without any special extended training. They are just taught for a few hours how to walk with crampons and use an ice ax in the event that they fall and start sliding off the mountain. They are then fitted with boots and sent on their way. Usually the plan involves a somewhat moderate hike to the base camp where they spend a few hours resting, then leave at midnight for the summit, hoping to reach it at sunrise and return back down a few hours later.

Jeffrey told me that he had climbed Rainier with his son several years ago and had a close call when he fell into a crevasse. Usually it is considered one of the easiest glaciated mountains to summit, as long as you train properly. But, what I had planned was considerably different.

There are actually several routes up to the top, some of them requiring very demanding and technical climbing skills. I was with a team that was attempting to climb the Kautz Glacier that involved scaling a monstrous ice wall at a very steep vertical angle. In addition, whereas the usual standard route can be done in a day-and-a-half, this route would require four days and carrying a 65-pound pack. Given that I only weigh 120 pounds, that was half my body weight!

I knew this climb would test me in ways I'd yet to consider. Once again, I considerably increased my training. Several times per week I would work all day teaching my classes at the university, then drive an hour to Mount Baldy, the highest local mountain at 10,000 feet. I would climb all night and get back down in the early part of the morning. I know this sounds a little crazy, but I was trying to train my body to get used to functioning at the highest level without sleep. Special Forces operators do the same sort of thing, and I was very much preparing to do battle.

Climbing a big ice wall on the
Mt. Rainier' Kautz glacier

My personal trainer emphasized that climbing is just as much about strengthening and preparing the mind as it is about doing the same for the body. I started watching a lot of movies about mountain climbing and reading books about accomplished climbers. I was especially impressed with Göran Kropp, a Swedish mountaineer who climbed Mt. Everest without oxygen or support of Sherpas in 1996, and this was after he rode a bicycle from his home all the way to Nepal! There was one part in his book where he talked about how sick he had become on the climb, coughing uncontrollably and being unable to sleep, yet he still reached his goal. I kept wondering if I had that special motivation and the tolerance for the pain and discomfort that it would take.

The same year that Kropp climbed Everest, there were many others who were caught in a blizzard and died. I read Krakhauer's book, *Into Thin Air*, which describes the 1996 disaster. Rather than dissuading or frightening me, I wanted to study the things they did wrong and make sure I didn't make the same mistakes. For so many climbers, getting to the summit is *everything* to them. They have something to prove. Unless they reach their goal, they feel like failures. So I was trying to consider ways that I could protect myself from danger as much as possible, or maybe I was just deluding myself.

One of the aspects of climbing that did absolutely terrify me, especially after watching all the films, was how they had to walk across ladders that were suspended over deep crevasses. They were walking in those heavy boots and spiked crampons, carrying all their equipment, literally suspended over nothingness. I made a note that I would have to practice doing that on ladders perched on top of tables.

Lakpa

I had set a date to climb Mt. Rainer during the 4th of July weekend. By the time the day of departure came around, I was terribly sick with a racking cough and fever. I couldn't decide whether to cancel or not, but eventually figured that if I didn't feel well enough, I could just stay at the bottom and rest.

Lakpa Sherpa, my favorite climbing guide, is perhaps one of the most accomplished mountaineers in the world, having successfully climbed Everest more than 15 times and led more teams on the mountain than anyone else.

Before I left for Washington, Jeffrey gave me a poster of a girl from Empower Nepali Girls. Her name is Sonisha and she lives near the Indian border. She is a beautiful girl and she lives close to where girls are trafficked into brothels, so I was terribly worried about her. She was only 12 years old when Jeffrey took her photo and now she was 18 and even more strikingly poised and beautiful. She was studying finance to be a banker, which is incredible, especially when you consider the isolated, poor village where her family lives. I decided I was going to plant the poster on top of Rainier—if I could make it to the top.

On the flight to Seattle, I looked out the window and I could see all the volcanoes looming above the clouds, Mt. Baker, Mt. St. Helens that blew its top off a while ago, and then majestic Rainier with its snowcapped glacier. Once we landed, I immediately went to the head-quarters of International Climbing to finally meet the people I'd been talking to on the phone all this time, to check out my gear, and meet my guide who was one of the most famous and accomplished climbers in the world.

Lakpa Rita Sherpa has summited Mt. Everest 15 times and he has been on 23 different expeditions, so you can imagine my surprise when I saw this little, skinny guy with the biggest, warmest smile you could ever imagine. He just exuded this quiet confidence, and I knew that I could immediately trust him with my life. I felt so honored that I would be going up Rainier with perhaps the greatest living climber in the world. I knew that he had successfully and safely led over 250 clients to the top of Everest, which is the world record. He was also the first Sherpa to summit all of the so-called Seven Summits, the highest peaks on each continent, including Kilimanjaro (Africa), Vinson (Antarctica), Denali (North America), and Aconcagua (South America) which I'm proud to say that I had already climbed. As warm, modest, and kind as Lakpa presented himself, I still felt pretty intimidated just to be in his company. I desperately didn't want to let him down.

This is Not Going Well. At All.

Once I tried on my loaded pack with all my gear, food, and supplies, I could barely hold myself upright because of all the weight on my back. Truthfully, I was freaking out, not only because I could barely keep my balance, but also because I was coughing so hard, it felt like my chest was about to explode.

It wasn't long after we began the ascent that I had to pee really badly. Of course whereas male climbers can just pull off to the side, undo a few flaps and zipper, and just let it go, it was a major pain for a woman to stop, loosen the harness, pull down all the clothes, all without a private place to hide since we were on an open glacier. I tried to hold it as long as I could until we could get to camp, but between the coughing and walking, it felt like my bladder was going to burst before we arrived. To make matters worse, everyone on the team was so much bigger and taller than I was, so I had to take much longer steps to keep up with them, tiring me further.

Not only did I make it to camp without an accident, but it was a beautiful afternoon. Once we set up our tents and rested a bit, we climbed higher to prepare the next camp since we'd be summiting that evening. Meanwhile I couldn't stop coughing and it was scaring me. I wondered if I had pneumonia or something even worse. There was no chance I would get any sleep, so I just lay in my tent trying to keep my lungs intact. I could tell that Lakpa and the other guides were worried about me and were thinking about sending me back down.

I found some solace thinking about Göran Kropp and all the ways that he suffered yet still persevered, and it gave me the determination to hold on as best I could. So what if I hadn't slept much in the last 72 hours? But I could tell the rest of the team had been looking at me and wondering if I was going to put them in danger because I couldn't hold my weight. I took Lakpa aside, showed him the poster of Sonisha, and told him why I was doing this. He is Nepali and I could see that this really touched him. Most of his clients are climbing for sport or diversion; he understood I was doing this for something so much bigger than myself, to help his people.

Sunrise

We woke up in the middle of the night. Or more accurately, everyone *else* woke up; I just stopped pretending to sleep. It was dark. There was no visibility. I was exhausted, a walking zombie, stepping, coughing, stepping, coughing, stepping. It was about 3 A.M. and I felt like I was going to pass out when I heard someone scream, "Ice! Ice!" That meant a piece of the glacier was falling down on top of us. Indeed, a big chunk of ice about the size of a bowling ball fell just past me as I hugged the wall we were scaling. I felt a piece of it hitting my helmet on the way down. My tent-mate was just below me and when she heard the cry, she looked up and got hit in the face, ripping her lip open. She yelled up to me that she was okay and could continue. Unfortunately, this was not the case with our lead guide who had been hit squarely in the face, causing a broken jaw. He insisted that he could continue anyway.

As we went higher, I was feeling weaker and weaker. When climbing on ice, the technique is to kick the front two spikes of the crampons into the wall at the same time that you swing the ice ax with your arm for added stability. We'd been doing this for hours and my arms and legs felt like rubber. I didn't have the energy to pull myself up any higher, so I was glued to the wall with others ahead of and behind me. I had no choice but to continue at this excruciating snail's pace.

I could see the sun starting to rise above the horizon, just a faint glimmer of dark brown that was turning orange and yellow. It was so incredibly beautiful that I forgot how tired and sick I was. It felt like I'd never seen anything so spectacular. Of course I *had* to take a photo. I took off my gloves, tucked them under my arm to reach for the camera, and then proceeded to watch the gloves tumble off into the sky. Drat! It was a good thing, though, that I had a spare pair of gloves in my pack.

The wind was picking up by then, and there was still a long way to go before we got to the top. I took a deep breath, dug in, kicked my spikes a step higher, swung my ax, telling myself just a little bit more, just one more step. I was trying to focus, but my brain was having trouble holding on to any thought. I considered what a relief it would be to just let go. I had no choice but to take the next step. And the one after that. Until. Finally. We reached the summit.

It turned out this was only the *first* summit. There were actually two of them and this was the "false" one, which I learned meant that there is a "real" one that was still higher. But once we regrouped and looked at our guide with the broken jaw, we could tell he was in trouble and we had to get him down to a hospital as fast as possible. His whole face was swollen and darkening.

*At the top of Mt. Rainier, the hard way, with a poster of
Empower Nepali Girls featuring an image of Sonisha, one of our
scholarship girls who is studying banking and finance.*

Before we began the descent, I took out the poster of Sonisha and
took a photo on what would be our summit. The wind was picking up
and ripped the poster out of my hands, sending it flying off into the sky.
This reminded me of the Buddhist prayer flags that you see all over the

Himalayas wherein it is believed that the symbols, incantations, mantras, and prayers of compassion are blown all over the world, spreading messages of peace. It occurred to me that now the spirit of our girls was blowing in the wind.

One More to Go

While the injured guide was escorted all the way back down to get medical assistance, the rest of us headed back down to our high camp to rest after the exhausting climb. After several hours of a grueling descent, we finally arrived back in camp. Or at least what *looked* like camp. The problem was that I was searching around and my tent was nowhere to be found. Apparently, either my tent mate or I hadn't closed the zipper all the way, and when the wind picked up, the tent, with all of our belongings, flew away like a kite, joining the poster of Sonisha blowing in the wind. All my brand new gear that I invested so much money in was gone. The only things I had left were what I was wearing on my back. No tent. No sleeping bag. No supplies or warm clothes. No way to get out of my wet clothes. Now we had no choice but to keep going all the way down the mountain because there was no way we would otherwise survive the night.

It was already the middle of the afternoon. We'd been climbing since midnight. I'd had virtually no sleep for three days and nights. I was coughing uncontrollably. I was so tired I couldn't even walk a straight line. The only good news was that at least with all my equipment blown off the mountain I didn't have to carry much. Buddhists urge us to let go of all attachments to things that might hold us down. Well, I sure had *that* going for me.

Lakpa was trying to keep my spirits up and keep me awake, so he started telling me stories about his life and his family, how he ended up settling in the U.S. His brother, Kami, was climbing K2 as we were speaking. It is the most treacherous mountain of all in that four out of every ten climbers who attempt it end up dying. I was struck by how incredibly humble Lakpa was, how it took a lot of effort to get him to talk about himself, and the incredible things he has accomplished. I made a vow to myself that in the future I would not climb any mountain without Lakpa at my side.

"So," I asked him, as we finally approached the end of our journey, "do you think I'm ready to climb Cho Oyu?" That was the next required challenge before I could be considered qualified to attempt Everest. It is the sixth highest mountain in the world at 27,000 feet, just 20 miles from Everest on the China-Nepal border.

Lakpa kept walking beside me, but he didn't say anything. I wondered if he heard me and I was feeling really nervous. If he said no, then my dream and plan were over. That was it, the end.

I heard him clear his throat and I turned to look at him. I saw that he was smiling and he shook his head in that characteristic, indistinct way that could mean, "yes," "no," or "maybe."

I held my breath again and waited for some elaboration. "Yes," he finally said. "I think you are ready. You have had many problems on this climb. With your sleep. And your cough. But I think you are ready."

I was elated and relieved. I wanted to scream with joy; however, I wanted to keep some semblance of dignity, so I just thanked him for all his support and help. As soon as we got back to our hotel, I passed out.

CHAPTER 9

—— ✀ ——

Sara: A Dream Come True

December, 2014

IT FEELS LIKE everything I've done so far in the mountains has been practice and rehearsal for the "real thing." Each of the climbs was targeted to test a particular skillset, whether acclimatization, conditioning, cold weather adaptation, rappelling, avalanche safety, and a bunch of other things that I had learned, if not mastered. But now I was about to attempt a monster, the mystical mountain the Tibetans called "Turquoise Goddess," Cho Oyo. Even Edmund Hillary couldn't make it to the summit because of dangerous avalanches, not to mention Chinese army troops spotted in the region. It might not be K2 or Everest, but more than fifty climbers have died trying to get to the top.

This was going to mean being away from my husband, Matt, for six weeks and I felt so guilty about that. He was still being teased so much by his friends for not keeping me harnessed at home. But he knew this was something that I had to do. But I've got to admit I'm really nervous about this, whether I can stand the hardships of that harsh environment being above 20,000 feet for so many weeks.

Mind and Body

One way I tried to manage my anxiety was to dramatically increase my training regimen. In addition to running up and down Mt. Baldy as often as I could, I included weightlifting, rowing, yoga, indoor rock climbing, running, swimming, and anything else I could think of. I knew that once you are above 7,500 meters, your body is so deprived of oxygen you start dying. You can't eat, can't sleep, and you start dropping weight. And since I don't weigh very much to begin with, I was doing my best to gain as much as I could—so eating was part of my training as well.

My guides and trainers had convinced me that preparing my mind was just as important as my body, so I also spent ten days at a silent meditation retreat center where we were admonished to surrender all cravings and to accept that nothing is permanent. I wasn't ready to embrace all of that, but it was good practice to work on my mind.

The part I was *most* excited about was that I'd be flying to Kathmandu first and would have a chance to meet the scholarship girls for the first time. Jeffrey had contacted the staff there to alert the children that I'd be arriving before we headed into China. He thought it would mean a lot to them to meet a woman who is a mountain climber. I asked Jeffrey what I should take with me for them, and he suggested just photos of my family and my life to show and inspire them. So I took my pictures of Iran, my apartment, my parents and siblings, my workouts in the gym, and the one of me holding the Empower Nepali Girls poster before the wind blew it away.

I also felt a little more reassured because I'd "met" all of my teammates now on social media. They seemed really friendly, spirited, and funny. I also learned there would be another woman going with us, Laura, who would be my tent-mate. She is a mother with six children and her goal was to climb each of the Seven Summits like Lakpa did. Remarkably, she had already scaled them all except Everest, which she had attempted to summit twice before, but had to turn back each time.

It turned out that Laura and I were on the same flight to Kathmandu, so I got a chance to connect with her at the gate at Los Angeles. I felt very reassured when I saw that she was as tiny as I am: we would be in this together.

So, THIS is Nepal!

This would be my first trip to Nepal, and I had no idea what I'd encounter except what Jeffrey had briefly told me. Upon arrival, the airport looked like it was unfinished, just a single building and one runway. I had heard the story about a plane that was stuck on the tarmac and the mechanics couldn't fix it. They flew in an expert from the manufacturer and he couldn't do much either. So they sacrificed a goat on the runway and, guess what? That did the job! The engines started right up.

My first impressions were that everything seemed dusty and foggy and there were people everywhere. Even though I've spent a lot of time in the Middle East, nothing quite prepared me for the version of Third World that exists in Nepal. Nothing seems to work quite right there with the constant strikes, delays, crazy traffic, power outages, political instability, and corruption, and yet everyone is so incredibly patient with it all. The people are among the most generous, kind, and welcoming that I've ever met.

The Nepali people make a gesture that I described earlier with Lakpa, where they kind of rock their heads side to side. At first, I thought when I asked a question they were saying, "No," to me, but then I thought it meant, "Yes," or even "Possibly." Now I realize it can mean any of these, but mostly it just means, "Sure, whatever you want." I found the Nepali people to be the most accommodating, easygoing folks you could ever meet with their glorious smiles. But the most charming thing of all is that you are constantly greeted by everyone—older people, shopkeepers, waiters, children, even babies, with "Namaste," which, roughly translated, means as I indicated earlier, "The spirit within me honors the spirit within you." It's accompanied by hands formed as a triangle under the chin as a demonstration of respect. I think the world would be a much better place if everyone did this instead of shaking hands.

The drive from the airport was like something out of a crazy movie. There were no discernable lanes of traffic. I'd see a motorcycle zipping by with a father driving, the mother sitting behind him, one child on the mother's lap, another barely holding on to the back, and then an infant perched on the handlebars. Another motorcycle zipped along with a goat on the driver's lap and a cage of chickens attached to the back. Almost just like back home.

On this particular day of my arrival, the driver explained that things were a little more congested and crazy than usual because it was a festival day.

"A special holiday?" I asked him. Laura wasn't paying much attention as she'd been to Kathmandu before, but she was staring out the window at a cow standing in the middle of the road blocking traffic. I also noticed there were police or soldiers standing around everywhere with machine guns, which I hoped weren't loaded.

The driver shook his head side to side, which I assumed was agreement. "Yes, it is a special holiday of Teej in which women pray to Lord Shiva for their husbands to have long lives. The women who are not yet married pray to Shiva that they might find husbands. . ."

"Wait a minute," I interrupted. "Only women do this for the men?" I wondered if this was the equivalent of our Father's Day.

"Yes, only women do this," he explained. "They wear red *saris* with *potes*—these are like glass, how do you say, seeds. . .no, beads that glitter. And they fast all day."

"Wait," I interrupted once again. "Are you saying that women starve themselves all day so their husbands will. . ."

He made that head shake again.

I paused for minute, taking all this in. "Well, what about a day for men to honor women, so that they may live a long life? When is *that* festival?"

The driver shrugged. "There is no such day."

Ah, just like back home in Iran where women are second-class citizens. I wondered what the local people would think about Laura and me, two women from America who were going to climb their biggest mountains. And I wondered what the scholarship girls would think of me, a woman who looks like them but is not at all interested in being subservient to men or devoting my life solely to my husband's long life. I am fortunate that Matt is as devoted to me, my career, and my interests as I am to him.

The Maze

Laura and I arrived at the hotel, surprisingly comfortable and reassuring after spending 24 hours crammed into airplane seats. Lakpa and another of our guides, Marvin, were there to greet and welcome us in the lobby, along with a few other members of the team who would be joining us. Before we even got settled, the guides were all about business, and they wanted to do a gear check to make sure we had everything we'd need for the climb. They didn't want to discover that once we were in the "death zone," above 8,000 meters where oxygen is less than 50% than it is at sea level, that we were missing some article that could literally save our lives. In my case, they weren't satisfied with the climbing pants I brought. They didn't think they would be warm enough at the below-zero temperatures we would be facing. Always generous, Lakpa told me that since we were the same size, he could just loan me an extra pair of his. I was so relieved because after losing all my clothes and equipment on Rainier, I didn't have a lot of extra funds left to buy more clothing. Matt was launching a new business enterprise in his field of cybersecurity, so we were on a strict budget.

After unpacking and showering, Laura and I decided to go off exploring in the tourist area nearby called Thamel. This is the place where a lot of backpackers, ex-hippies, and trekkers on a budget hang out for cheap food, shopping, and seedy drug deals. Once we walked over there, it really did remind me of what I imagined things must have been like during the 60's. There were lots of young people, mostly from Europe, wandering around. Every few steps, some shady characters approached us to sell their wares. I was greatly amused, but I could tell Laura was just annoyed by all the people trying to sell us stuff—incense, little toy instruments, even hashish. Jeffrey told me that one time he was walking through here with a friend and a woman approached them with an infant, thrust the baby in his friend's arms, and started to run away. Jeffrey's friend had to run to follow the woman to give the baby back. Apparently, the woman was so poor that she imagined her child would have a much better life with this foreigner. He also warned me of all the scams in which a woman and a baby might approach us, ask us to buy her some milk and food for them, thank us gratefully, but then after we leave, return everything back to the store because they were hired by them to reel in the tourists. But hey, I'm from the Middle East and I was used to these tactics

Thamel is my kind of place. It's crazy. It's crowded. Pedestrians, cars, scooters, bicycles, rickshaws, were everywhere on the narrow streets that were more like alleyways. Shops were crowded everywhere with the owners calling out. There was the wafting smell of incense and weed, the sounds of Tibetan and Hindu music chants blaring from speakers. You could purchase anything here, and I loved the bargaining with the people, although Laura didn't much like it so she asked me to do our negotiating. I've had plenty of practice in Tehran so I demonstrated my favored technique. The guy tells you his price and you offer half of that. Then when he cuts it only ten or twenty percent you act disgusted and start to walk out of the store. Very slowly. When he calls out to you to come back, you ignore him and continue on. But slowly so he can catch you. Then you tentatively agree to come back inside, perhaps have a cup of tea. And so it goes. It's all about the process, not just the price. This is a sacred tradition, one in which I am both comfortable and find endlessly amusing.

I'd been in Nepal only a few hours and it felt like home to me. I loved the people. I loved all the activity. As we walked along the narrow alleys, taking in all the sights and sounds, Laura and I started comparing notes on our prior climbs. Although she had much more experience, I realized that my own upbringing and culture allowed me to be her teacher as well, while we navigated through this maze.

Holding Back Tears

Jeffrey had made arrangements for Pasang Tempa Sherpa, the President of Empower Nepali Girls in Nepal, to pick me up and show me around the next morning. The first thing that struck me about Pasang was his distinctive laugh. The thing that strikes *everyone* about Pasang is his laugh—frequent explosions of delight at almost everything, all the time, even at the most inopportune moments. There was a whole language to be translated from his laughing that I soon learned to decode. Sometimes it meant something was truly amusing, but other times it could mean so many other things. Almost everything he said was punctuated with a laugh. This was just about the friendliest guy I'd ever met, but also the most knowledgeable about his country. Jeffrey told me much about him as they have been working together for over a decade, first as his guide and later as the head of the foundation in Nepal.

Although Pasang supports his family as a trekking guide, he also devotes a considerable part of his life to helping our girls, along with Babita, a social work student who is both a scholarship girl as well as a staff person for the organization and pretty much runs things, along with Pasang, his family members, and friends. Babita has a room in Pasang's home along with other volunteers and even several scholarship girls who have nowhere else to live.

Pasang was accompanied by several children, including his daughter Chhusang, age 16, and Nimsang, the little girl I mentioned earlier that he had found abandoned on the street. While we were driving back to his home, the girls asked me if I was familiar with any famous Nepali or Indian actresses. There was an instant bond between us because growing up in Iran I was indeed quite knowledgeable about Bollywood songs, so we started singing together the whole way. Pasang just kept laughing while he pointed out sights along the way.

Finally, we arrived wherever we were going—this was never quite clear to me. I saw these two big, blue doors that started to open as we got out of the car. We had been driving on this bumpy, rocky road, squeezed between walls that were so narrow that only one vehicle could squeeze by at a time. I looked through the doors of what I figured must be the entrance to a school, and saw two long lines of children that had formed. They were organized by age and size with little ones, perhaps only 3 or 4 years old standing first. I could see they were all holding out their hands with flowers in them, and as I walked through this gauntlet, each child placed flowers in my hands or a *khata*, a sacred scarf blessed by the Dalai Lama, around my neck. Each child greeted me with *Namaste*, or "Welcome, ma'am." I couldn't help but break out in tears of joy. You just can't imagine what it feels like to be so honored by children you haven't even yet met.

Apparently, the children had been told who I am and why I was there. They knew I was an engineer and a mountaineer who was going to climb Everest, but they'd also been told I'm a volunteer and fundraiser for the organization that is raising money to support the poorest girls in their school. I was trying to smile and show my gratitude to the children, but all I could think to do was to keep telling myself, "Don't cry. Keep it together." I just wanted to stop and hold all the children. I wanted to tell them that I would do my very best to help them. It felt like my whole life was changing in that moment, that I would never be the same. So far, everything I knew about these girls and what the foundation was doing was second-hand from stories told to me by Jeffrey and others. But now this was real. I looked at these girls' gorgeous, smiling faces and realized that their actual lives depended on me. I know this sounds overly dramatic, but trust me, if you had stood among all these smiling children, you would have felt the same. It was impossible to hold back the tears.

Sharing My Story

I sat in a circle with dozens of the scholarship girls, the oldest perhaps 12 or 13, as well as younger ones who couldn't have been more than 4 or 5. Babita introduced herself to me, and I was surprised how poised and in charge she was. Pasang had gone off to huddle with the school principal and teachers, leaving us alone. It was Babita who organized everything, and I could see the girls adored her. She was the model of everything they wanted to be some day.

I was asked to tell the girls about myself, so I explained where I come from and what my job is in America, that I teach at a university, and that I'm an electrical engineer and computer scientist by training. I could see that some of the girls weren't exactly sure what to make of that, how a woman who looked like them could have a man's job. Then I told them about my plan to bring greater attention to their needs by first climbing Cho Oyo, followed by Everest. Some of the girls' mouths dropped open, immediately covered by their hands; others just giggled as if this was some kind of fantasy story.

Babita asked the girls to introduce themselves to me, and it wasn't at all what I expected. They had memorized a simple introduction in English. "My name is Amita. I am in Class Three," one girl would say. "My parents' names are Amaya and Sunita. I have two brothers. Their names are Sandesh and Sajit." As they would recite this carefully rehearsed speech, they would look down at their feet because they were so shy.

One of the most important parts of our program is not just providing financial support for children's education, but also mentoring and fostering ongoing relationships between the girls and professional women who talk to them about future career opportunities.

I squatted down by each one of them and said, "Please look at me. Don't look down. Be proud of who you are. You are smart. You will do great things. I will help you." As I was saying these words I felt so shy myself. I felt so overwhelmed and out of my element. I didn't know what I was supposed to do or say. Jeffrey hadn't prepared me for this part.

After we went through this awkward series of introductions, I started showing the girls some photos that I'd brought along. When I pointed out my husband, Matt, they all started giggling. But by that time, the ice seemed to have been broken and they started asking me questions about how I had become an engineer, whether girls can do that in America, and why I wanted to climb mountains. Jeffrey had already told me that, except for Sherpas who are specifically paid as guides, most Nepali people don't really understand why tourists and trekkers come so far just to walk in the mountains. For them the trails are the only highways to get from one place to another, and they are grueling, steep, difficult to navigate while carrying heavy loads. It doesn't strike them as much fun.

The girls seemed particularly intrigued with mountain climbing expeditions and why I did that sort of thing. I thought for a long minute before answering. "Well," I said after the long pause, "unless we push ourselves to do things that are really hard, and face challenges that frighten us, we can never really know what we are capable of doing. Do you know what I mean?"

I saw their heads nod. I wasn't sure, at first, how much English they actually understood, but I could see absolute clarity in the faces of the older girls. "Climbing mountains," I continued, "is about facing hardships for me. It's a way for me test myself."

Again they nodded, or rather waggled, their heads. This time I could tell they agreed.

"Many people have told me that what I do is not the sort of thing for a girl to attempt. They say it's too hard and that I should stay home with my husband and have babies."

The girls covered their mouths and giggled, but I could tell immediately that they got it, the message I was telling them. They gathered around me even closer, a few of the little ones competing to sit on my lap, some others leaning over my shoulders. I wanted them so badly to know that they could do this, too. They could follow in my footsteps and pursue their own dreams.

They asked so many wonderful questions. How did I come to the United States? What was it like living in Iran when I was a child? What was my husband like? How did I go to university and why did I decide to study engineering? What did I think of their country so far? I laughed at the last question because I'd been in Nepal for less than 24 hours, but I patiently answered anything they wanted to know about me. They were especially surprised that I didn't get married until I was 30 years old and didn't yet have any children. I explained that first there were things I wanted to do in my life, that I hadn't gotten married until I finished my education and had a good career. And, I didn't want to have children until I first finished other things in my life that were important to me. I could tell that this interested them but sure didn't fit with their own cultural values in which girls as young as 15 years old might be expected to marry, and hitting 18 without a husband must seem strange to them.

"There's no hurry," I told them. "It's better to finish your education so you can take care of yourself and your family *before* you get married. That way you will never be dependent on a man."

One girl, who looked about 14, piped up after that. "Excuse me, Ma'am. But I have friends and know other girls who have boyfriends and they want to get married. My father, he tells me that I should get married too. He says that girls don't belong in school anyway. What should I do?"

I had no idea what to say to her. I know Jeffrey fields these kinds of questions all the time and has been doing this for years. He's a psychologist and all, but I'd only been here a day and I was used to solving problems as an engineer. I had no solution to this problem. All I could think to do was waggle my head the way that they do it, saying, "Yes," "No," and "Maybe." I needed time to figure that one out.

They were all staring at me, waiting for some other gems of wisdom, so I told them more about my life when I was younger. "Although I'm now 33 years old, when I was younger I fell in love with a boy."

Again they tried to stifle their giggles as they looked at one another.

"There is much pressure in my culture, too, for girls to marry when we are young. But there are many things I wanted to see and know, and I knew those experiences would end once I was married."

One of the older girls suddenly stood up, as if she was about to leave. "Well, my parents want me to marry my cousin. They are forcing me and there's nothing I can do about that." Then she turned and walked away.

It just broke my heart, but I tried to keep my attention on the girls still around me.

It seemed to be intermission when one of the teachers in the school came by with a tray of cookies and a thermos of the milk tea, their national drink. Everywhere I would visit in Nepal, we would be offered variations of this tradition, whether it was tea with milk, *Chai* tea with various spices like cardamom, cinnamon, and ginger, or *Sherpa* tea with the even more unusual ingredients of yak butter and salt.

I was starving because it was lunchtime and I hadn't yet eaten anything because of the 12-hour time difference from back home. The children politely refused the refreshments for reasons unclear to me other than I was their guest, so I shoveled down a few cookies, gobbled the mug of tea, and then turned back to them. "How about let's play a game? I've noticed that when you introduced yourself to me, you were very shy. Your voices were so soft I could barely hear you. And you memorized something to say to me, but it probably wasn't what you really wanted me to know about you. So, how about this: Everyone stand up and form a circle. When I point to you, I want you to look me straight in the eyes and speak up. I want you to use a loud, confident voice and tell me something about yourself that is important. I don't care what it is, anything you want. And you can tell me in English or Nepali, it doesn't matter. I don't care what you say, but I want you to say it loudly, confidently, looking at me the whole time."

Hey, I was just winging it. I was used to teaching college students, mostly all men who were studying to be engineers, so this was *way* out of my own comfort zone. To my surprise, they *loved* this game. Every time I pointed to one of them, they would talk to me in a strong voice. Most of the time I had no idea what exactly they were saying to me, but they had fun doing it. I realized that although I had come to Nepal to climb Cho Oyo, already, after just one day, it felt like I'd already accomplished enough that I could have gone home a happy woman.

We took "selfies" of one another, and then a group photo, before I had to say goodbye. I promised I would return to them in six weeks after I climbed the mountain.

Home Visits

Before I returned to my other world of climbers waiting for me at the hotel, Pasang and his family took me out for a meal to try *dal bhat* for the first time. This is the national dish, rice and lentils, usually accompanied with curried vegetables, that Nepalis eat twice each day. It's often the *only* thing they eat because it is considered so nutritious and inexpensive. Let's just say it is an acquired taste.

Pasang and Babita had arranged for me to visit a few more of the scholarship girls in their homes. They thought I might like to meet some of the families and to see how the girls live. The first place we stopped was a small hut, maybe the size of a small hotel room. There was a young mother there, maybe late teens, and she had two little girls who were 3 and 5 years old. When I asked where the father was, the mother just shrugged. Apparently he had gone to an Arabic country to find work and was never heard from again. They didn't know if he had died, or had simply abandoned their family. This was a very common scenario in which hundreds of thousands of people from Nepal are exported to Qatar, Dubai, and other countries to do manual labor that the local citizens consider beneath them. The workers are restricted to camps and risk their lives in construction or maintenance jobs in 120-degree temperatures every day in order to send money home.

We walked to another house where there was an 8-year old scholarship girl. As we sat and talked, she told me she enjoyed math as her favorite class., I asked if I could see her schoolwork. This girl was so, so smart, like a little jewel hidden away in this desolate, little hut with no resources. The scholarship girls are children who consider the opportunity to attend school and study as a privilege. In Nepal, unlike in the United States and other countries, students must have a uniform and school supplies, plus pay tuition to attend even public school.

While I was sitting with the family, I had this vivid flashback of being back in Iran. I remember I was about 10 years old and it was the Persian New Year. There was a knock on the door of our home and we were sitting around because there was no school that day. I opened the door, and standing there were some of my teachers. I was so surprised

I just stood there with my mouth open, thinking I was in some kind of trouble.

"May we come in?" one of the teachers asked, seeing my look of surprise and confusion. I just nodded my head and shyly backed away. Thoughts were racing through my head of all the things I might have done wrong. I just knew that I must have done something really bad for all of them to come to my house like this, especially on a holiday.

Several times each year our staff, volunteers, and team members, make the rounds to conduct school and home visits of every one of our scholarship girls. This often takes months to complete, given the remote locations of several of the villages where the children live. During the visits, we sit and have tea with the families and neighbors, review the girls' homework, and talk to everyone about the importance of providing support for education.

I couldn't have been more wrong. The teachers just wanted my parents to know how smart I was and what a capable student I had become. As we sat and had tea together, just like I was doing with this girl in Nepal, they asked me all sorts of questions about my life, what subjects I liked best, and every little detail about our house. I remembered that so vividly as I was sitting in this hut, and I recalled what a huge impression that had on me for the rest of my life. That was one of the first times—maybe *the* first time— that I realized I had a special gift, one that my teachers wished to support and nourish. It meant so, so much to me and it made me want to work even harder.

Now I was the one who was trying to inspire and support this girl who was so incredibly gifted as well and didn't quite realize it. I could feel myself starting to lose control, so I abruptly excused myself and ran outside sobbing. It was as if this little girl was me—and I was her. I realized in that moment that I might have the same impact on these children as my teachers once had on me by showing how much they cared and supported me.

When I came back inside, pretending I had had to use the toilet, I was composed once again. I turned to the mother and thanked her for being so strong and for supporting her daughter's education. "You must be so proud that she is so smart. She is going to do important things in her life with your help, with *all* of our help." I explained to her that we were going to support her in school as far as she could go. We would provide a scholarship and enough financial support that she could continue her education to study engineering like me, or perhaps medicine.

The mother held up her hands to her chin in the familiar sign of respect, and she broke out in the most glorious smile. "*Dheri dhanyabahd*, thank you so much for giving my daughter something that was never given to me." Then she reached out to hold my hands.

This conversation and experience were repeated a half dozen times that afternoon. In each case, the family welcomed me with tea and biscuits. I visited these homes where five people lived in the space of a large closet, sometimes the parents and one child sleeping together on a pallet on the floor. The kitchen was just a little portable stove on the ground. I reminded myself that I would never have the right to complain about anything in my life ever again.

By the time we returned to the hotel, I was an emotional wreck, not to mention exhausted from the time change and the overwhelming day. While my teammates were enjoying a day's rest shopping, touring the city, loading up on pizza and beer, I had been immersed in this invisible world that climbers and trekkers never see, never know exists. But there was no better "training" I could ever have done to prepare for the next 45 days in the Himalayas. Now I *knew* why I was doing this. I had a reason that dwarfed anything else I could ever have imagined. When things got tough, when I wanted to give up, I would just remember these girls and how much they were depending on me to bring attention to their plight. It was now my life's mission to be their role model, to show them what a woman can do.

I found it interesting that I had come all this way to help and inspire these children. I visited their homes and their school to tell them what I would do to help them. But it turned out that they had done as much for me. I felt like I found something within me that I'd been missing. I now had this sense of mission and purpose. I felt so clear about the direction I was going, a place that I hoped the girls would follow to accomplish their own goals and dreams. I felt so, so grateful, so much energy. I felt happy, fulfilled, satisfied. I felt complete.

CHAPTER 10

꙳

Sara: Crossing Borders

August, 2014

THE MONKEYS WERE not only aggressive but downright vicious. I was with several of my team members visiting Swayambhunath, a Buddhist temple and ancient Tibetan monastery that sits atop a hill in Kathmandu overlooking the whole valley. This particular temple is not only known for its architecture, scenic views, and thousand-year-old history, but also for its permanent residents, which are hundreds of hungry, rather territorially possessive primates. For some reason that escapes me, they are considered holy and are pretty much left to their own devices. They just run wild, steal food right out of your hands if they can, and have even been known to snatch backpacks or cameras from the hands of unwary tourists.

Several of us formed a protective circle around our bags, hoping to discourage the monkeys from further attacks. Laura, my roommate and tent mate, was with me, along with several others who were part of our international team, including Henri from France, Ted from England, Kyle from Virginia, Jiban, our trip coordinator and logistics officer, and Marvin, our lead guide. This was my one and only day to look around the city before we began our long journey into the mountains, and I was already enjoying the companionship of our group, all such interesting, adventurous individuals, not at all like so many of the cautious, risk-adverse people back home.

Long Drive

The distance between Nepal's southern and northern borders is less than 100 miles, and from Kathmandu to the Chinese border is just a few dozen miles. However, with the narrow, treacherous mountain roads that are often washed out by landslides, or closed because of accidents, it can sometimes take days, rather than a few hours, to traverse the country. Looking at the map, it seemed like we could arrive at our destination before lunch, but I hadn't anticipated all the frequent delays when we left early the next morning.

At one point, close to the Chinese border, there was a landslide that washed out the road which was now indistinguishable from the river that had been running alongside it. I was feeling so nauseous I would take any excuse to get out, walk around, and catch my breath. This time, though, the road was completely blocked, there was no way to get through at all. We were forced to abandon our vehicle and find another on the other side of the blockage. We had to unload all of our stuff, carry it through knee-deep mud, and then repack everything in our new transport. It amazed me not so much that there was chaos everywhere, but rather that our guides were so casually adaptable, as if this sort of thing happens all the time—which I suppose it does. This was all new for me, so I started to complain about how muddy, hot, and humid it was, and how disorganized things seemed to be, until I learned that more than 200 people died when the side of the mountain buried a nearby village. It reminded me once again to slow down and just take things in stride the way the Nepali do.

This laidback attitude was even more evident when we reached the border and there was a bridge stretching between the two countries. On the Nepal side, the guards were just standing around smoking, chatting, laughing, goofing around, but on the other side of the bridge we entered a very different world. The soldiers were all standing at perfect attention, outfitted with enough weapons and equipment to go directly into battle.

"Your papers," one guard said to us. No smile, no "please." Just a bored, stern face and a hand extended impatiently.

Then, the border guards started going through our stuff looking for contraband, which I assumed must be drugs or weapons. "Books," one soldier said to me, and I looked at him with confusion.

"Books?" he repeated. "Do you have books?"

I wasn't sure how to answer that question. Of course I had books with me. I was about to spend six weeks stuck in the mountains, so I had all kinds of reading material with me and I couldn't imagine surrendering them or else I'd be stuck staring at the roof of my tent all day and night. So I just shook my head, hoping that was enough.

There was a whole gauntlet of additional searches, with each guard a specialist it seemed in searching for certain things, the last of which checked my temperature. I hadn't been examined so thoroughly since I visited my doctor. This place was worse than Iran.

The Chinese confiscated some of our food and equipment—I don't know why—probably so we were forced to spend money to buy all the same things once again to boost their economy. I wondered if we would find our own possessions on sale when we went shopping at the next village.

We had already ascended 10,000 feet, and yet the landscape reminded me of the desert back home. All the trees and waterfalls had vanished as we arrived in the next village where we would spend the night. Instead of worrying about aggressive monkeys, we were now warned to be careful of the wild dogs that barked and growled at anyone nearby. Besides the dogs, the only others around were chain-smoking locals engulfed in clouds of smoke, and other climbing teams headed in our same direction.

At first I was anxious and uncomfortable without access to any communication to the outside world. No Internet or email. No social media. No news. The little television in the motel only seemed to pull in one channel screening a show that was called something like "China's Got Talent" and featured little kids doing all kinds of strange things. We were completely insulated in our own little universe. It was during my stroll through the one and only dusty street, searching hopelessly for Wi-Fi, that I spied a huge, wooly monster following me. When I speeded up or slowed down, the animal seemed to match my pace, as if measuring me for a snack. It took a few minutes for me to figure out that it was my first sighting of a yak.

Preparations and Training

Each day we were scheduled to do acclimatization hikes at progressively higher altitudes. It was during these walks that I got to know my group members a bit better. I had been a little worried because I had noticed that a few of the men were so much taller and bigger than I was, requiring me to match their longer strides during climbs. But before long, I was reassured that we would all take care of one another.

It's the stories you hear while on a climbing expedition that partially make the suffering so endurable. Several of our guides had scaled many 8,000 meter peaks all over the world, escorting fabulously wealthy clients and eccentric adventurers. They regaled us of tales about one older guy in his 60s who fell in love with a 20-year-old and decided to divorce his wife while on the trip. Another rich guy decided he was worried about how his heart would hold up, so while on an Everest expedition he decided he needed to see his cardiologist back home in Los Angeles. Once he was examined and told his heart was just fine, he hopped back on a plane, flew back to Kathmandu, and then hired a helicopter back to Everest Base Camp. Now *that's* some acclimatization trip, going from sea level to 18,000 feet in just a few days.

We moved on to the next village still higher, and it was just as peculiar. This time instead of having to worry about rabid, wild dogs or angry, stalking yaks, we were besieged by children who begged for money. If we didn't offer some bribe, they would attack us with vicious kicks or throw things at us. It got to the point it wasn't safe to walk around alone, so we had to travel in packs for self-protection.

The routines for each day as we ascended higher and higher toward base camp were much the same. Long hikes during the day, then descend back down and sit by the stove and dry our socks. There was plenty of time to think about things, about life, about priorities, about loved ones, sometimes way too much time. And yet there is something altogether different when on a climb like this. Back home, at least in Southern California, everyone is busy all the time with their work and responsibilities. People live so far from one another that it absolutely rare that friends and family

132

get together and just hang out, without the distractions of a television or mobile device. Sitting in teahouses, there was really nothing else to do but talk to one another about our lives, our past adventures, our future plans and dreams. It was during these conversations that I shared with others why I was actually doing this climb, not just to prepare for Everest, but to show all our girls what is possible if you are willing to work hard enough.

First View

I woke up really early one morning, way before sunrise, because we'd been told that if it was clear, we would be able to see the north side of Everest. Of course I'd already studied every contour of the mountain on maps, Google Earth, and photographs, but for the first time I could actually see the fabled peak that was calling to me.

We left that day for Base Camp which I expected would look like a village of mountain climbers, but instead resembled an army camp with Chinese soldiers standing around with their guns and giving orders not to take photos. We pretty much ignored them: What were they going to do, shoot us?

As we toured the camp, I could see the summit of Cho Oyu with its distinctive flat top looming high above us. We made the rounds visiting the tents of the other climbing teams from around the world, and I was surprised to meet another Iranian, a doctor from San Francisco, who was just as shocked to see me.

"What are *you* doing here?" he blurted out. "Shouldn't you be at a shopping mall looking for boots and a leather jacket?"

I supposed he didn't mean to be so rude, but he was talking about the stereotype of Persian girls from wealthy families in Southern California. He seemed to thaw a bit when I explained to him why I was really there, not for myself, but to help others.

There was even more free time at Base Camp than in the teahouses because we needed recovery days after climbing high to further acclimatize. And when you are staying in a tent city, there isn't much privacy since you are all living virtually on top of one another. To keep ourselves entertained we'd ask each other questions about our lives, such as, "What's the worst thing that ever happened to you?" or "What have you done that gives you the most pride?"

Thinking about the first question, I told the others about a time I was visiting family back in Iran. It was during a presidential election, with the usual corruption and protests about the rigged outcome. I was hanging out with some friends while we walked down the street when all of a sudden we could see police and soldiers running toward us, launching tear gas grenades in our direction. One of the policemen started to attack me with his baton, chasing me as I ran away. I eventually escaped and hid until things calmed down. As I told this story, I looked around at the others sitting at our table in the dining tent, wondering what they were thinking about me. I could tell that the Nepali guides were nodding in understanding because they have had similar experiences during the ten-year civil war, but I didn't know what the others would think about this woman from Iran whose life was so different from theirs.

That evening there was a full moon on a perfectly clear, cold night. As I was laying in my tent, I could see the shadow of a yak so close that it looked like he was standing right outside. I thought about opening the flap to look outside and see if I needed to take defensive measures, but I was too scared to move. So I just stayed up all night gripping my ice ax in case I needed to protect myself.

Up and down. Up and down. That was my life. We'd climb higher and higher, conditioning our bodies to the thin air and steep climbs, and then descend back down to rest and recover. During one of our frequent social gatherings, a few people at the table asked me what I was going to do next. That always seems to be a frequent topic of conversation among climbers, no matter what mountain you are on—what are you going to do after this one?

At first, I was reluctant to admit my plans because I didn't want to hear any more doubts and criticism from people. But I'd come to like and trust my group; they were accepting and understanding toward anything that anyone chose to reveal about themselves. So I confided to them that I was on Cho Oyu to prepare for Everest. Laura was already aware of my plans because we'd stayed up late at night talking in our tent about all kinds of things, and I already knew that she was thinking about Everest next year as well. We'd even talked about possibly doing it together if our schedules worked out.

After my disclosure, almost everyone else said that Everest was a dream of theirs as well, but one they admitted was likely unrealistic given the exorbitant cost and the amount of time they'd have to take off from their jobs. Lakpa and Marvin then started telling many stories about their Everest climbs and how different it is from what we were doing because of the special equipment and gear that was needed, how much more difficult it would be because of the Icefall, the ladders, the sheer numbers of other climbing teams that were all competing for priority on the ropes. I remained mostly quiet during the discussion, listening as carefully as I could, but I could tell that some of the others looked at me differently after that—they could tell this wasn't just a casual lark for me, but a mission I was taking very seriously.

Laura and I were becoming quite attached to one another, quite literally. Sleep at high altitude is intermittent and sketchy at best, and I constantly woke up several times in the middle of the night, that is when I could sleep at all. Sometimes I found that during the night I would roll over and was practically sleeping on top of Laura, or somehow I ended up on her side of the tent. More often she was so sweet and kind, I didn't have the heart to tell her that we were all tangled up, so I reassured her that she was the best tent mate ever. You just can't imagine the things you have to put up with being crowded into such close quarters. Depending on what one has for dinner, the farting can be so out of control you can barely gasp for air in the already limited oxygen available. Sometimes we had to leave the tent flap open to get some air circulation going, but then because it was so cold outside, we would be freezing all night.

Before we headed much higher to set up another camp, I was able to call Matt on the satellite phone. I missed him so much and, once hearing his voice, I told him that it made me want to come home.

"No, no!" he insisted, "you can't do that. I've told so many people what you are doing and I'm so proud of you. You have to make the summit. Then you have to do Everest."

I just started crying because he supports me so much and won't let me give up.

Advanced Base Camp

My climbing style is, to be perfectly honest, a little unusual. I like to listen to music while on the mountain, especially favorite Persian songs that are so irresistible that I can't help but dance in the middle of my steps. I move my arms in that hypnotic rhythm and stutter-step my feet in a very rough approximation of moves I can make easily without heavy boots and crampons. I don't ever realize I'm doing this, but the others on my team are usually quite amused by it. Sometimes, when I'm alone on top of a ridge, or *think* I'm alone, I'll turn up the volume and really start moving and swaying to the music.

As we headed to higher elevations, I could definitely feel myself becoming stronger, so far so good. We stopped at a teahouse of sorts at 17,000 feet, more like a little hut with tent fabric extended over it. The woman taking care of the place was very pregnant and had an adorable 3-year-old sitting on her lap. Her husband (or brother?) approached me as soon as I was settled on a chair and asked me if I was married, then if I had children at home. When I responded affirmatively to the first question, and negatively to the second one, he looked at me very carefully, and asked if I might like to take their child back to the U.S. with me. I honestly couldn't tell if he was joking or not, but when he saw my startled look, he walked away.

I was already uncomfortable in the hut because of a putrid smell. The only source of fuel they have at this altitude is yak turds. They take a pie, flatten it out, dry it in the sun, and then use it for heat and cooking. Not surprisingly, it smelled like shit, and all I could think about was getting out of there, away from the odor and the confined space and the father staring at me. But it was so cold outside we had no choice but to remain inside.

The next day, as we hiked up to ABC, Advanced Base Camp, Marvin carefully checked each of us out, asking how we were doing, assessing our fitness and readiness to go so much higher. Most of us already had headaches and insomnia. Laura, in particular, hadn't been sleeping at all.

"How are *you* doing?" Marvin asked, when it was my turn.

I hesitated before answering. I was actually doing quite well, all things considered. But I didn't want to just give him a stock answer and tell him I was just fine and feeling strong. Since others were complaining of various ailments and discomforts, I felt guilty just saying that everything was perfect, so I told him that my kidneys felt a little tender. Big mistake.

Marvin jumped on that right away, and I could see he was becoming angry. "That's because you don't drink enough water. I keep telling you to drink more water but you don't listen!"

At this point I couldn't tell him I was lying, that my kidneys felt fine. He was right, in one sense, in that I'm not the most diligent water drinker, but my body seems to function quite well without becoming dehydrated. One thing that men don't understand is how much harder it is for a woman to pee in the mountains. Men can just pull down their zippers, whip it out, and spray designs in the snow. It's hard enough for women to have to undo their climbing harnesses and pull down their pants in the frigid temperatures, but there's absolutely no privacy. At night, when it's too cold to go outside, we are forced to use a funnel in one of our extra water bottles. But I wasn't about to explain any of this to Marvin, or defend myself in any way. I just nodded sheepishly and took a long gulp from my bottle to show him.

Marvin still wasn't satisfied. Even though I understood he was concerned about my safety and health, I still felt really hurt and I tried to hold back tears, which he either chose to ignore, or didn't see.

"Look," he said, driving his point home once more, "unless you start drinking more water, I'm not taking you to the top. Understood?"

I turned away from him abruptly and walked off by myself because I felt so humiliated. This was so unfair because I had made up the problem in the first place just so I would fit in with everyone else and so he would have something helpful he could tell me.

Finally, the guides told us we had arrived at the destination, but I had to take their word for that because I could barely see past my own goggles. One minute it was still and quiet, the next brought a blizzard. The wind suddenly picked up at ferocious velocity, followed by a blinding snowstorm that was coming at us more horizontally than vertically.

As soon as we stopped, I unpacked every item of clothing that I carried with me, layering all my fleece and my puffy jacket and pants. Even outfitted like a big balloon, I was still wet and freezing. I walked around in the increasingly deep snow, as much to stay warm as to tour our new home. I could see that the porters from another team had set up tents already, while all of our equipment and supplies were arriving by yaks a few hours later.

We were graciously invited by members of the other team to warm ourselves in one of their tents, and they offered us hot drinks. As usually happens in such situations, we traded stories with one another about where we'd been and where we were going next. There was one woman climber with the other team, Christina, who seemed especially interested to know who I was and what I was doing. When I told her about our work supporting the girls, and that I was climbing to raise money for them, she wanted to know everything about our program. I noticed, at this point, that everyone else had stopped talking to listen to what I was saying.

I looked around the tent at the 30 other climbers who were all watching me with interest when I described what I'd been doing 10 days ago, visiting the children in their homes. I would later learn that literally thousands of climbers pass right by some of our scholarship girls standing along the Everest trail (easily recognizable with their bright puffy jackets that we provide for them) and hardly anyone ever stops to talk to them.

The group seemed so interested in what I was doing, or perhaps they were just happy to be talking about anything other than the weather, the routes, and complaints about the food, cold, and inevitable delays. It was during one of the pauses that I heard one voice ask me fairly aggressively, "Aren't your parents worried about you?"

Of course it was the Persian doctor from San Francisco who I'd met earlier.

"Excuse me?" I said, dumbfounded about where *that* came from.

"Your parents. And your husband. Do they let you climb mountains like this?"

"Let me?" This guy was really getting under my skin. Or maybe I was just annoyed because he reminded me of so many other men from back home.

"Yes. I know Persian parents. And I don't think many of them would be happy about you doing this, being here."

I so badly wanted to ask him if his parents or his wife let him climb mountains, but instead I just smiled sweetly and ignored him. The timing was perfect when one of our guides stuck his head inside the door to tell us that our stuff had arrived.

Heaven and Hell

I was surprised to learn that there was enough space and supplies for each of us to have our own private tent while we stayed at advanced camp. I wasn't really happy with that. I actually preferred sharing with Laura because we could talk to one another and keep our spirits up, especially when one of us was feeling discouraged. I was still upset about my conversation with Marvin, so I asked to talk with him after dinner.

"You know, earlier, when I told you my kidneys hurt?" I began uncomfortably.

"Yes, of course, I hope you will take me seriously when I tell you. . ."

"That's the thing," I interrupted him. "I wasn't actually being honest with you."

"What do you mean?" he asked me, suddenly on alert. "Are you having other problems? Are you. . ."

"No, no," I tried to explain. "Quite the opposite. You see, my kidneys aren't really hurting."

"They're not?"

"No, I just said that because everyone else was complaining about something and I felt badly because I'm feeling really good. I'm sleeping well. I don't have headaches like the others. I'm feeling strong."

He just shook his head and walked away. I don't think he believed me. But as he turned away, I promised him I'd drink more water.

The next day was a leisurely recovery and rest day, and the weather cooperated with the plan. It was spectacularly sunny and gorgeous, and at our exalted altitude, we could see the Himalayas spread out across the horizon. I decided to do some laundry and wash my hair, which made me feel more content than I could ever remember feeling. I had everything I could possibly want in this moment. "This is it!" I thought to myself. I felt so relaxed, so complete, so present in the moment. My brain was completely silent; there were no thoughts at all, no feelings except the exhilaration of being exactly where I was. I felt like if I had died right then, I would have died happy.

My goal that day was to drink as much water as possible, and to do so with Marvin around so he could see I was listening to him. At one point he asked me specifically how much I'd consumed so far that day, and I proudly told him that I'd already finished almost two liters. He broke out in a huge smile and gave me a high-five. I could tell that he was only concerned about me. If that's all it took to make Marvin happy, it was no big deal. But I also noticed that Lakpa seemed different, not his usual effervescent self, as if he was worried or annoyed by something. This was worth monitoring. He takes care of all of us, and so many other people in his family and friends. I wondered who takes care of him?

Imagine lying awake all night, headache pounding, nauseous and exhausted,
staring at the ceiling of your tent. Climbing big mountains involves the most
spectacularly amazing experiences of a lifetime, with the most remarkable views
on the planet, but it also involves a fair bit of suffering and discomfort from
the cold, the physical demands, and the 50% reduction of available oxygen.

I don't know if it was the altitude, or just that we had not exerted ourselves during the day, but I had no appetite for dinner. And now I had a headache that was so bad I couldn't sleep. Feeling exhausted and depleted the next day during our acclimatizing hike, I was a wreck. My headache was becoming worse and I had absolutely no energy, barely shuffling along. Even drinking lots of water didn't help.

When we returned to camp several hours later, I went immediately into my solitary tent and started crying. If the day before it had felt that I had arrived in Heaven, today I was in Hell. For the first time, I thought to myself that I didn't want to be there anymore. I wanted to go home.

I'd had enough. I just wasn't strong enough to do this. The headache was driving me crazy, like it was crushing me, and now I could feel a sore throat coming on. I felt nauseous and once again had absolutely no appetite. I was trying to remember what I'd even eaten that day, but my head was throbbing so much I could barely remember where I was, much less why I was here.

"A thousand times bigger." That's the mantra I kept repeating to myself. "I have to become a thousand times bigger than myself." It was a reminder that I wasn't here for myself, but for the girls. This was only suffering. Suffering was only an annoyance.

It's one thing to say that, and quite another to believe it. The reality was that everything was so difficult up here. Peeing, pooping, eating, changing clothes, even finding things in my bag, were so aggravating and ridiculously challenging. All the things I took for granted and did so easily back home were absolutely exhausting on the mountain. As I lay in my tent, feeling sorry for myself, thinking how badly my clothes smelled, I finally fell asleep listening to music at a soft volume so it wouldn't further aggravate my headache.

CHAPTER 11

———— ✂ ————

Sara: The Pee Bottle

September, 2014

MY THREE WATER bottles had become the most consistently visible way for me to measure time. Perhaps Marvin was right when he warned me to keep drinking water; maybe if I'd been more diligent about staying hydrated I wouldn't have suffered so much with acute altitude sickness. I'd been experiencing the classic symptoms—insomnia, headaches, nausea, and light-headedness. At least I wasn't yet spitting up blood.

The best cure, naturally, is prevention. And one of the most reliable ways to do so is by drinking lots of water. So that was now my mission. And I became obsessed with filling and refilling my liter bottles, and often I would catch Marvin nodding at me approvingly. Unless things improved, the only other option was to descend in elevation—and after working so hard to gain this altitude, there was no way I was going back down again until after we reached the summit.

A Prayer to the Gods

I felt a little better the next morning, although I had still barely slept, or at least it felt that way. My headache seemed less bothersome, although I could still feel dull pressure. I wasn't sure if I was improving or just getting used to tolerating the discomfort. So much of climbing is about putting up with pain.

Since we were soon to begin the serious climbing, we had a Puja ceremony scheduled during which we were instructed to beseech the gods for safe passage. This is a Sherpa tradition, especially among those of them who are monks. It is sometimes the case that an eldest son might be sent to a monastery as a child for religious instruction and to serve the lama, the spiritual leader. If economic hardship within the family becomes untenable, the monk may then be granted permission to earn money as a guide to help support family. There were several such Sherpas in our group who would lead the ceremony.

There had been a small alter created, wrapped in colorful prayer flags. As the monks chanted their prayers, we were each asked to reverently place our crampons and ice ax on top of the rocks in order to bless them for the climb. I also placed the flag of Empower Nepali Girls on top and made sure it was clearly visible. Then we presented symbolic gifts to all the gods respected by those present, Hindu, Buddhist, Christian, Muslim, among them. Incense was burned and then we each threw a handful of rice as an offering. As a last part of the ceremony, we rubbed flour on one another's faces as a personal blessing. We thought this part was pretty hilarious since we now resembled ghosts.

I realized as I was watching the proceedings that this wasn't really about climbing at all, or even some superstitious belief that this would somehow protect us from harm. This was a ritual about respect for the mountain, about the uncertainties of life, and about reflective meditation about the meaning of our actions.

Walking Zombie

Today we were carrying some of our stuff to Camp One, 21,000 feet. I planned to leave as much behind as possible in my tent to lighten my pack that was already way more weight than I could comfortably manage. It took us 10 hours to get there and back and the whole time it was snowing. The last hour before we arrived at Camp One, I was seriously regretting my decision to lighten my pack because I was freezing with limited clothes. I decided to forget about the summit; I just wanted to go back down. Every second I was asking myself, "Why the hell are you doing this?

Go back down." Every single step, I was trying to convince myself to take just one more before I turned around.

I was so tired that at one point I felt an abrupt jolt and realized that I had actually fallen asleep as I was walking! I realized how dangerous this was because there were so many deep crevasses crisscrossing our route, and one small mistake would send me careening down into noth-ingness. By then I was seriously concerned because I wondered how I would recover from such a lapse of attention as we got higher, the slopes steeper, and the dangers becoming so much more frequent.

In and out of my reverie, which at times felt like hallucinations, I started thinking about an older woman I'd read about, 64 years of age, who managed to swim from Cuba to Florida. She had to deal with so many horrible things during the 110-mile marathon that took something like 50 straight hours in the water. There were huge waves she had to swim through, blowing winds, stings from numerous jellyfish, the threat of sharks, not to mention having to exert herself like that for two straight days. It seemed insane, especially considering how old she was. But she was my inspiration and I imagined her watching me. I could also almost hear her talking to me, encouraging me to keep going. "Remember," I could hear her saying inside my head, "you picked this goal. Nobody made you do this. It's bigger than you. This isn't about you anyway. It's for the girls. Remember why you are doing this. Remember the people counting on you."

I'd like to say that this counsel made all the difference, but whatever inspiration and encouragement I felt from the ghost of this woman living inside my head lasted only a few steps longer before I thought about giving up once again. Then I remembered what it was like on Aconcagua and how finally reaching the summit was one of the best days of my life. Sure, it wasn't nearly as hard as this monster, but that experience reminded me once again why the goal was so worth the effort. For some reason, I was able to hold onto that feeling until we finally reached the high camp.

A More Positive Attitude

After descending back down that first climb up to Camp One, we were given a rest day to recover and, wow, did we need it. Almost everyone had headaches, sore throats, and flu-like symptoms. I had totally lost it trying to get up to 21,000 feet, so I wondered how I could possibly handle another 6,000 feet. I think at that moment, if I had the strength to get out of my tent, I would have tracked down Marvin or Lakpa and insisted that someone escort me back down. But that would have required more energy than I could muster, so I just wallowed in my misery and hoped I could fall asleep.

During the night I dragged myself out of my sleeping bag, completely forgetting that I had decided to quit the day before. Although I hadn't gotten much sleep, this time it wasn't because of fatigue, aches and pains, or the altitude. I had transported and left some of my gear at Camp One, including my pee bottle, the one I use during the night with a funnel so I didn't have to leave the tent and brave the frigid cold. I remembered Laura saying that holding your pee brings down your body temperature. Because I was under strict orders to keep drinking water, there was no way I'd be able to hold it in during the night, which required me having to go outside at about 2 AM. I opened the tent flap, crawled outside, and looked up at the most spectacular view I'd ever seen, stars so bright and numerous that they blanketed the sky. I was so taken with the experience that I started to go back into my tent until I realized I had forgotten why I was out there in the first place, to pee.

By this point I had been outside long enough that I was absolutely freezing, and the prospect of pulling down my pants was not very appealing. I thought of just going back inside and holding it until morning until I realized that peeing was the least of my worries. I had the worst stomach ache and diarrhea, so whether I liked it or not, I was going to have to strip down and take care of business. I also realized I had to get some sleep because we were heading back to Camp One in the morning and that would become our new base of operations. I found I was actually looking forward to that because it meant I would get to share a tent with Laura again. I didn't like being alone.

Once settled back inside, waiting for sleep to hit me, I started reviewing all that I had learned these last years about keeping a positive attitude, especially during adversity. Mountain climbing is as much a mental effort as it is a physical activity. It's about tolerating difficulties without feeling discouraged. It's about staying disciplined and focused. But mostly it is about staying upbeat, especially when things get really, really tough. I realized that if I could do this, if I could really drag myself up to the summit, anything else I did in life back home would be easy by comparison.

The really strange thing was how mercurial and unpredictable my moods had become. One minute I was ready to surrender, and the next I was feeling fearless. I was in the throes of ecstasy watching the spectacular stars at night, then a bit later I was crying myself to sleep because I was so miserable. I needed to somehow stay more grounded and to stop being so upset with every little obstacle along the way. I needed to keep more positive energy flowing so I practiced my meditation as a way to relax and remain clear. The next thing I knew, it was morning and I'd had the best sleep I could ever remember having in a long time. I felt renewed and bursting with energy. My cramps were gone. No more nausea or headache.

Notebooks from Beyond

I suppose there are a lot of possible explanations for my recovery. Perhaps it could be explained that my body had finally adapted to the altitude, or I'd finally gotten the rest I needed, or whatever malady infecting me had run its course, but I preferred another theory. I'm not a conventionally religious person. In some ways I'm quite skeptical of orthodox traditions, which you could certainly appreciate growing up with all the oppression by religious leaders in Iran. But I have always believed in some kind of divine or spiritual power that emanates from somewhere in the universe.

I don't mean to sound all New Age, but I remembered one incident that occurred when I was studying at the University of California, Los

Angeles. I had little money and very few resources in college, so I lived in one of the dumpiest apartment you can imagine. The building was such a wreck that the windows wouldn't open and hardly anything worked properly. I didn't even have any furniture, and I could barely afford to eat anything other than noodles.

It was my first day of classes and I hadn't yet figured out a way to buy any supplies for school, including notebooks to record lectures. I showed up at my first class and sat next to a girl who had a collection of a half-dozen, color-coded, seemingly customized notebooks in bright primary colors. When she saw me looking curiously at her stack of books, she just shrugged. "It's my Dad," she said apologetically. "He bought them for me."

I turned away, wishing I had a father who would help me get settled in school. During the previous few days I saw so many parents helping their kids move into their apartments, taking them out for meals, walking with them around town while they shopped for things. My family was back in Arizona and couldn't really help me with anything, so I was completely on my own. The girl noticed I had nothing on my desk, so she asked me if I wanted one of her notebooks. I just shook my head and tried not to cry. I felt such deep sadness and thought of my father, my real father who died before I was born. I imagined that if he was here with me, he could take me out to buy notebooks and other things I needed. For now I'd have to make do with the few sheets of paper I had borrowed from the girl next to me.

After class I was walking back to my dismal apartment when I heard this noise that startled me. It was the "beep, beep" sound of a truck backing up, and I saw that it was pulling into an alley just in front of me, blocking my way. I had been so lost in my own thoughts, feeling sorry for myself, that I almost walked smack into it.

This guy got out of the truck and, for a minute, I thought he was going to yell at me for almost getting hit by his truck. But instead, he walked around to the back of the truck, opened the door, and started yelling in a loud voice, "Notebooks. Free notebooks. Who wants some notebooks?"

Are you kidding me? This was awesome! What I wanted most in the world at that moment were notebooks and who pulls up but this guy offering to give away free notebooks. And for no reason that I could figure out, unless they were advertising something they wanted to distribute. But hey, beggars can hardly complain.

"Hey, I'll take one!" I yelled out to him. I was so excited I could hardly stand it. This was downright weird and it was about to become much more so.

"Take as many as you want," he said to me with a smile, and placed a pile of them in my arms, all different colors. But here was the *really* amazing part. I glanced at the cover of the notebooks and saw emblazoned right in front the words, "safari.com."

That's my name! Of all the coincidences imaginable, not only does this guy show up with a truck of notebooks, just when I needed them, but it was as if they were specifically designed just for me! It was spooky. But it also renewed my faith that forces beyond what we can possibly understand appear during those times of our greatest need.

I know this sounds really strange, and I'm a little embarrassed to admit this, but I I felt—no I knew—that these notebooks were from my dad. I started sobbing as I walked home, and I said a prayer to my long dead father who I'd never actually met. "Thank you, Father, for taking care of me. Thank you for being there for me when I needed you the most."

So as I woke up from my first good night's sleep, feeling completely refreshed, almost reborn, I just nodded to myself in acknowledgment. I don't know if this time it was my father's energy or a guardian angel that had shown up again, or those in my meditation group back home, or Matt sending his love and support, but *something* was very different, and even though I couldn't explain it, I was very grateful.

The Ice Cliff

It was like I was vibrating. And it was two o'clock in the morning. I'd eaten so many protein bars and B12 vitamins that I doubted I would ever sleep tonight with all the energy in my system. It was now official: I'd be sleeping, or at least resting, at 21,000 feet. You never really sleep at this altitude anyway; you just pretend to yourself. And if you do manage to slip off for a little bit, you end up gasping for the scarce oxygen after an hour or two.

My knees were still vibrating from the caffeine I'd consumed, or the lack of oxygen, or excitement, or something else. It was scaring me because they wouldn't stop wiggling, as if they had a life of their own and weren't even connected to me at all. I wondered if I should wake up a guide and tell him what was happening. Maybe it meant I was dying. I tried to listen to music to calm down, but the battery was dead because of the cold. I took the battery out and put it in my underwear to try to warm it up. After about a half-hour, I tried again and it lasted long enough to play one song. It was 4 AM but we still had hours to go.

This was the best time for me to poop since everyone else was sleeping. During the day there was no choice except for me to squat out in front of everyone else with my pants down around my ankles. People could see my butt no matter which way I faced. There's nowhere to hide, no trees, no rocks, just flat open space on our little ridge. That's why I so enjoyed those moments alone in the dark, but I would have liked them a lot better if I hadn't been literally freezing my ass off. I stayed out there staring up at the stars long enough that, once again, I lost track of what I was really doing there and so I tried to focus. I'll tell you this, though: one of the unsung pleasures of life is to wipe yourself with a snowball. It's bracing of course, but it feels mentholated and soothing, kind of a wake-up call to that end of your body. It felt so refreshed once I was bundled up again.

The night seemed endless, but finally it started to get light, and I knew we had an important day ahead of us. For the first time, we would be tackling the most technical part of the climb, an ice wall that required us to use our crampons and ice ax. It was slow going for sure, especially because we needed time to get into a rhythm and work as a team. Much of the way, all I could think about was the chocolate bar

I had been saving when I needed it most: *this* was going to be that special occasion. I was actually hungry for the first time in a while. I had skipped dinner because they were serving MREs (meals-ready-to-eat), which are what soldiers eat when they are on the battlefield. They were so disgusting I just settled for a handful of almonds and I couldn't wait to get at the chocolate bar.

After several hours of climbing, we took a break to rest for a few minutes. I immediately took off my pack and started digging into my bag for the treat, setting things aside, balancing one of my two water bottles on the ledge while I searched further. Success! Just as I grabbed the chocolate bar at the bottom of a pocket, my pack touched the water bottle and I watched with horror as it tipped over the edge and rolled down the glacier. Lakpa, always quick on his feet, started to run after it, but then thought better of the idea when the bottle picked up further momentum and slipped down into the clouds.

Shit. Shit. Shit. That bottle was still half–full, and water is absolutely crucial to survive at this altitude. I could see Marvin shaking his head and looking furiously at me. I called out to him, "Hey, don't worry. I've still got another one."

I did indeed have another liter bottle in my pack, but it wasn't the one I thought it would be. Instead of bringing a second bottle of water, I had mistakenly packed the bottle that I pee in at night. Oh, my gosh, I was so embarrassed. And Marvin was making things worse, accusing me of doing this on purpose for some reason, although I couldn't figure out why anyone would deliberately jettison a water bottle that was necessary for survival. While Marvin was threatening to send me back down, Lakpa jumped in and offered to share his bottle with me.

Marvin was still furious with me on the way down. "I read your file in the office about your first trip to the Cascades."

I just kept my head down and continued walking, hoping he'd just leave me alone. I felt badly enough as it was.

"It said that before then, you had absolutely no mountaineering experience whatsoever. I have no idea what you think you are doing here on an 8,000-meter climb. It took me fifteen years of training and experience to get to this point. But now you show up and think you can do this after a year. What were you were thinking? Why did they even let you come on this expedition?"

I thought of all the things I could have said in response, but I could feel the tears starting to fall and I didn't want him to know how much he was hurting me.

"Look," he continued in a scolding tone, "I'm the one in charge of this team. Don't you ever think you can go to Lakpa and that he'll help you. If I say you're done, that's it, you're done. That means you go back down. Do you understand me?"

I nodded.

"I said do you understand?"

I'd had time to regain my composure. My goggles were starting to fog up from the tears, so I lifted them up onto my helmet and turned to face him fully. "Yes, I understand," I told him in a voice that was surprisingly steely and calm. "That's the reason why I'm climbing with you. Because I trust your expertise and experience. And I know you are just concerned about my safety." As I said this I was smiling, I suppose because I was nervous and upset—and that seemed to just enrage him further.

"See, right now, you're just smiling at me. Like you don't take me seriously."

I tried again. For the life of me I couldn't figure out why Marvin was so mean and on my case all the time. I told him one more time that I appreciated his help and suggestions, but he still didn't seem to believe me. He just shook his head and walked away, ignoring me all the rest of the way down.

Good Cop, Bad Cop

"He's just always on my back," I was telling Laura, still upset and crying while we were talking in our tent. "What the hell does that even mean, that I smile when he talks to me, or that I don't take him seriously?"

Laura was trying to calm me down and take care of me, just like the big sister she had become to me. While I lay on my bag feeling sorry for myself, she helped me take off my boots and climbing gear.

"And *now* what am I going to do with only one bottle for water, plus my pee bottle? I don't even know where my extra bottle is; I thought I left it in the tent." The tears started flowing once again.

We talked for a while longer, and then I knew I had only one option left: I would have to drink out of my pee bottle, which had the most putrid smell of old, fermented urine. I could even see yellowy crust along the bottom that seemed impossible to scrape out through the narrow opening at the top. I tried putting snow inside and rubbing it around but it didn't seem to help much. I was going to have to drink pee water for the rest of the trip, and that seemed the absolute end of my self-control. My only saving grace, one that would earn us all a respite, was that the Sherpas had more rope-fixing to do on the steeper parts ahead of us which meant we would have to descend back down to Advanced Base Camp.

One of our team members, Kyle, was also not doing well at all. He'd completely lost his appetite and was wasting away, already having dropped 15 pounds. Kyle was getting perilously close to the absolute limit. I had also heard that the only woman on another team was forced to quit, and I felt sad about that as well.

Once we arrived back at ABC, I tried to regroup. I washed my clothes, and tried to disinfect the pungent scent from my pee bottle. The good news was that once we descended back down to 18,000 feet, it felt to me like sea level compared to where we'd been. I felt strong once again as we started back up to Camp One, followed by another grueling day back on the ice cliff. Whatever optimism I had temporarily entertained was crushed yet again once we got off the wall, and I could barely walk back to camp without falling. Lakpa, who still took a special interest in me, reached into my pack to remove some of the items and put them in his own pack. This time when I cried, it was with such love and appreciation for his incredible caring and support.

I felt like I was being bounced around like a ping pong ball by the classic good cop, bad cop routine. One reason I had been feeling so dispirited, besides the physical exhaustion, was that while we were climbing, Marvin noticed a small mistake I had made with the rope, and he started scolding me. I guess it's a cultural thing in that Nepalese in general, and Sherpas in particular, are just so incredibly patient, supportive, and kind, very different from the arrogance of American climbers, or at least the few of them that I'd encountered. For reasons I didn't understand, Marvin just seemed to hate me and resent my very presence on the mountain. It felt like he was always looking over his shoulder, waiting for me to make a mistake so he could jump on it and humiliate me. I'd just never encountered anyone like that since I had been a child in Iran.

A Flood of Tears

Once resettled in Camp One, we headed up to Camp Two, which was astoundingly flat. I'd seen videos of climbers who were stuck sleeping in tiny tents the size of a refrigerator box, literally attached to the side of a cliff, buffeted by high winds, so I didn't imagine we'd have level ground to settle ourselves. That meant, however, that there'd be absolutely no privacy for pooping, so Laura and I would have to use the vestibule of our tent, a one-meter area inside the outer flap.

There was yet another conflict with Marvin one morning during break-fast. Ted had asked me at the table what my husband, Matt, does for a living. I was explaining that he owned a cybersecurity business when Marvin interrupted me.

"You're married?" he asked.

"Of course," I answered. "You didn't know that?" And I started to continue my explanation to Ted when he stopped me once again.

He looked at me quizzically. "I already asked you once and you told me you weren't married."

He was accusing me of lying or something, when Ted entered the conversation. "We all know she's married," he said. "She talks about Matt all the time."

Marvin just shook his head in that annoying way. Again, I wondered what this was all about? Was he jealous of me in some way? Or disappointed that I'm married? Whatever. I had to let this go because I already had enough to worry about without constantly wondering what he was going to say and do to me next. It got me thinking that so much of everything we do, whether at work or climbing a mountain, is related to the ways we get along with others. I felt so fortunate to have such a wonderful group of people with me, so I just had to accept that only one asshole was within usual limits.

Finally, after breakfast, we were told that this would be our last rotation before reaching the summit. We would head back up to Camp One, then on to Camp Two, and then still higher to Camp Three, the last stop before the top. We were all so excited, but also lost in our own thoughts about whether we would make it after the others had given up.

The going was definitely easier this time going back up to our Camp One. We were on our way to Camp Two, almost to the ice cliff, when Marvin approached me with his characteristic scowl. "How much water are you carrying?" he asked in a challenging voice.

All I could think to myself was, "Don't smile. Don't smile, whatever you do." I knew I was on solid ground, so I told him I had the regulation two bottles with me.

"Show me," he said, and I was stunned that he didn't believe me. Why on earth would I lie about something like that? Even more curious, why would I deliberately only carry one bottle when I knew it would put my life in danger? Did he actually think that I would do such a thing just to show him he couldn't order me around? It was crazy.

I reached into my pack and pulled out the first bottle, and then the second one, almost defiantly.

"What's this?" he said in a voice so loud that others began gathering around us. He was pointing to my second bottle, which was about three-quarters full.

"What do you mean?" I was totally confused.

"I mean you are a liar."

"Excuse me?"

"You're a liar. You lie about everything."

At this point there were more than 30 climbers watching this exchange, all of whom had stopped to rest at the same spot. They were all watching this interaction with curiosity.

"Are you serious?" I asked him, absolutely stunned. Just because I had already consumed a little bit of the water from one bottle, he was saying I had lied to him. This was utterly ridiculous. It was my turn to become furious. He was humiliating me in front of my friends and fellow climbers.

"Why do you hate me so much?" I asked.

"What do you mean?" he responded.

"Why do you give me such a hard time? Aren't you supposed to be *helping* me, not breaking me down?" If he thought my smile was disturbing, he must have loved my look of complete contempt.

"That's it," he said. "You're done here. I'm not taking you any further."

Just when I was about to totally lose it and go off on him, he stomped away, leaving me alone. Everyone else who had watched this scene pretended to ignore what happened, but for me this was the last straw.

I followed Marvin and screamed to his back, "I'm done. I'm tired of your crap."

"Fine," he said with this look of triumph. "Go back down."

"No, I mean *you*. You've been hired to take care of me, to help me, not humiliate me. How dare you speak to me this way, call me a liar, and in front of all these people. You are the worst guide ever!"

At that point Ted came between us. "Okay guys, calm down. It's okay." Then Marvin gave me a scornful look and walked away.

After that it seemed like people were avoiding me. Even Laura was nowhere to be seen. Maybe they thought I was infectious. So I walked alone for the next few minutes, tears streaming down my cheeks. I was just grateful it wasn't cold enough for them to freeze. I once remembered the story of the first woman to walk to the magnetic North Pole. And one of the greatest dangers she faced was being stalked by polar bears. She had a dog with her who would keep the bears at bay, but there were times when she wanted to give up and the tears would start, which was even more perilous because at those temperatures if she gave in to crying her eyes would freeze shut and then she'd be done.

With the warmth of the sun reflecting off the snow, there was no risk of my tears freezing, so I just let myself go. When I saw Lakpa walking back toward me, I tried to compose myself. I knew he would say the right thing and comfort me, but this time he surprised me.

"Why are you crying?" he asked. "Crying doesn't fix anything. You must stop crying. You're losing your body's water."

Well, I suppose he was right. But I found that comment absolutely hilarious, and I started laughing like a madwoman. Then, once he left me alone, I started crying all over again.

A Long Night

Once we arrived at Camp Two after another exhausting day, Marvin was high-fiving everyone, saying, "Good job, everyone!" Everyone but me, that is. I went inside my tent to hide and I dissolved into more tears. A few minutes later, Marvin stuck his head inside asking me if I wanted to talk about what was going on.

"Sure," I said. "I'm totally open to whatever you want to tell me to improve my skills, but I don't appreciate you scolding me all the time in front of everyone else. If you have something constructive to offer me, I would like you to do it in private. And I also don't like that you called me a liar. That's twice you've done that."

To my utter shock, he immediately apologized. "Look, I'm sorry I did that. From now on, I'm not going to criticize you. I *do* know you've got this. You've already made it to Camp Two and you are still strong. So I'll do my best to stay out of your way." With that, he ducked outside the tent, leaving me alone once again to my tears. I was dumbfounded by his change of attitude and apology.

Laura tried her best to calm me down. "Climbing this damn mountain is hard enough," she reassured me. "You certainly don't need this additional aggravation. And you can always climb with another company and never see him again." She was referring to the likelihood that he would also be the head guide assigned to my Everest expedition that was scheduled next.

I wish I could say that this made me feel better but I was still feeling sorry for myself, and so I cried myself to sleep once again. I just felt so miserable, so misunderstood, and so alone. I had never realized that the hardest part of the climb wouldn't be the mountain itself but rather all the interpersonal undercurrents and dynamics that were involved to reach the summit.

I later woke up in the middle of the night and felt like I was going to explode I had to pee so badly. But it was so frigid outside there was no way I was going out there. In turned out that Kyle descended early, enabling me to inherit one of his extra water bottles. So, now I was back to peeing through my funnel into my old faithful one. Unfortunately, my legs felt like rubber from the day's journey and I could barely support myself above the funnel. Before I knew it, my legs collapsed, knocking over the bottle half-full of accumulated urine, which spread all over my sleeping bag and clothes, including the heavy socks I was supposed to wear the next day. Still worse, because I was so dehydrated—even with my consumption of the prescribed water ration—my urine was brown with the most disgusting toxic smell. It was as if my body was trying to rid itself of all the accumulated poisons, the collective result of poor diet, inadequate oxygen, and psychological torture.

I just squatted there, staring at the mess, watching Laura sleeping and wondering, *What the hell do I do now?* There was no way I was waking up any of the guides and subjecting myself to more scolding. All I could think to do was to put on the piss-soaked socks, hoping they would dry sometime during the night in my similarly soaked sleeping bag. When I compared how miserable that night was, to the one I spent on Mt. Whitney that fateful night when I thought I was going to die, it was pretty close to a tossup.

The next morning the socks were still damp. I had no choice but to wear them. I certainly wasn't about to tell anyone, even Laura, about my calamity. I just couldn't take any more criticism and I'd lost hope that I'd get sympathy from anyone.

Summit Attempt

By the time we arrived to Camp Three, I had rediscovered some of my passion and excitement. It was a glorious day, absolutely clear and crisp. In every direction I could see snowcapped peaks rising above the valley far below. We were on top of the world, as high as I'd ever been, not only in terms of altitude, but spiritually and emotionally as well. I felt giddy and pure. I also felt strong, really strong and confident for our summit attempt early in the morning.

All the concerns and frustrations of the previous days just seemed to melt away. Even my piss-soaked socks had eventually dried, although when we resettled in camp for a few hour's rest and I removed my boots to massage my feet, I could smell the wafting aroma of the worst combination of scents imaginable. Even that couldn't dent my elated mood.

We watched the sunset, tried to eat something, and then retreated to our tents to get some rest before our wakeup call around 11 PM. Laura and I were so excited we knew that sleep would be impossible, so we lay quietly next to one another and listened to each other's breathing, which had by then had become so familiar and soothing.

I must have dozed off for a little while because before I knew it, I heard the wake-up call telling us to get ready. It was terribly cold, even with my down suit that is rated at minus 40 degrees. Surely it couldn't be *that* cold, I wondered. But on this morning, I decided nothing would poison my mood.

Lakpa was the lead guide and I was positioned right behind him, with Kami, his brother, right behind me. I was sandwiched between two of my favorite Sherpas, once again as if the spirits of the universe answered my call. Even better, Marvin was the "sweep" guide, all the way at the end of our team and as far away from me as possible. By that point I couldn't even stand looking at him. Once again, it felt like the gods had answered my prayers.

I could see a long line of lights sparkling in the distance all the way up the mountain. These were other climbing teams that had left before us, hoping to avoid the crowds. We were now using oxygen to assist us, which made things so much easier, but even with the flow adjusted for maximum capacity, there would be limited time we could rely on the assistance, especially with all the climbers ahead of us who might slow us down.

For the first time we had to do some seriously vertical rock climbing which, at this altitude, was truly exhausting. Lakpa could see me struggling and called out to me, "This is the hardest part. Once we get through the rocks, the rest will be much easier."

I just nodded, unable to talk intelligibly through the oxygen mask.

Climbing rocks with crampons and heavy boots is quite challenging, the spikes squeaking and scraping along, barely providing any kind of purchase. It felt like any moment I'd lose my grip. I could see Lakpa watching me carefully and I knew Kami was right behind me, providing some reassurance. I just hoped I didn't fall and take them both down with me since we were connected by ropes.

There was one team in front of us that was climbing without oxygen and they were going much slower than our pace. We were all connected to one another by the same guide rope, so that meant that in order to pass them, we had to unclick ourselves, pass around them, and then reattach ourselves. It was during those few minutes we were dangerously vulnerable to a fatal fall without a net. One slip and I'd be gone, possibly pulling the others down with me.

After nine hours of steady, relentless climbing, just as we approached the summit, I could see the sun beginning to peek out, and for the first time I could see all the ice and glaciers around us. There were 20,000-foot mountains all along the horizon, but they were dwarfed by Cho Oyu, which is the tallest among them on this side of the border. However, the first thing I noticed when we reached the top was majestic Everest rising still further into the sky; it was so close I thought I could almost leap over there. Next to it was Lhotse, which was almost at eye level with me. I turned around and saw all the prayer flags flapping in the wind. There is just no way I can possibly describe the feeling of exhilaration in doing something so incredibly difficult wanting to give up a hundred times, yet still forcing myself to endure all the hardships and continuing anyway. Two years ago I'd never in my life been in the mountains, or even camping, and there I was, standing at 27,000 feet. It was like an out-of-body experience, almost like I was weightless. I felt so, so thankful for the opportunity to experience this, no matter how difficult it had been to get to this point.

There isn't much time to celebrate once you reach the summit of a Himalayan peak. You are standing at the same height that planes fly along the jet-stream. It's absolutely freezing, 30 degrees below zero. The wind is blowing at 50 miles an hour. At best, you've got just a few minutes to take in the experience and then you have to get out of there before it's too late. So I took out the banner of Empower Nepali Girls that I'd been carrying with me all this time. I stretched it out between my arms, trying to hold it steady so it wouldn't blow away like the last time I had tried to do that. I asked Lakpa to take a photo for me so that I could show the girls when I returned to Kathmandu and the villages.

I took out my own camera to capture the moment, the spectacular views: the damn thing was frozen, the battery dead. I had anticipated that possibility so I made sure to keep my phone inside my jacket to keep it warm as a backup. I checked the battery and found it registering 100 percent, but after taking just a few photos, it also died. No matter: I tried to burn these unforgettable images into my brain. I remember reading somewhere that when you take a photo of something, you are actually *less* likely to remember the experience since your brain somehow knows not to waste memory space holding onto a visual artifact that has been recorded elsewhere. I don't know if that is true or not, but I did often find that taking pictures interrupted the primacy and intensity of a significant experience. So I just gazed around in awe, trying to hold onto these precious moments that I had worked so hard to earn. Truthfully, the whole scene was so improbably spectacular it seemed like it wasn't real.

Standing on the summit of Cho Oyu

The Long Way Down

Once again we were reminded that often the most dangerous part of a summit climb is on the way down. Only 15 percent of the climbers who died on Everest perished while heading up to the summit, the rest died on the way down or when turning back. People are exhausted and sleep deprived, having been on their feet already for 18 hours or longer. The chronic lack of oxygen impairs cognitive processing, so poor decisions are made. Legs feel like they are about to collapse. It's much harder to navigate downward steps when sometimes you can't see where you are placing your feet. Inevitably, mistakes are made. So we were warned, in spite of our exhilaration in having finally reached our goal, to use caution and care as we descended.

Once we returned to camp, all of us safe, I tried to rest for a few hours. You'd think that after 48 hours with virtually no sleep I'd fall unconscious immediately, but a few hours later I was awakened by some foreign spirit that seemed to have entered my body. My legs were vibrating of their own volition, as if they had a mind of their own. I was shaking so bad it felt like I had absolutely no control. I know this sounds amusing but it was actually quite terrifying. I actually wondered if I was dying, that my body was literally falling apart. I had a racking cough that hurt my chest every time I let loose. My muscles, my joints, even my internal organs, ached for relief. I took pain-killers but they didn't seem to put a dent in the misery, so I just lay in my bag for hours, hoping the suffering would either stop or kill me. It was the single worst night of my life. I now realized the price I had paid for this experience.

The next morning, all of us tried to engage in a celebratory mood, but most of us could barely walk. Much later, once we descended through Camp One and arrived back at Advanced Base Camp, we were more inclined to enjoy what we'd done. We held a special ceremony to honor and thank our guides and porters, tipping them generously for their courage and support.

We reversed course, passing through the same villages and teahouses we had seen during the beginning of our journey, but everything looked and felt different. *We* were different. We had been strangers to one another a month earlier and now we had shared some experiences that couldn't possibly be described to anyone, even though Jeffrey and I are doing are best to do just that. I just can't do justice to describing how hard this climbing is, even though we've given you an idea, nor can I really explain or defend why anyone in her right mind would ever subject herself to such terrible suffering.

Unfinished Business

After we arrived back in Kathmandu after successfully climbing Cho Oyu, I was over the moon excited about my prospects of tackling Everest next. I was a physical wreck, and still quite emotionally wounded from the interpersonal drama on the mountain, but I was also feeling more optimistic than ever about continuing my mission.

There was, of course, one significant piece of unfinished business and that was getting together with Marvin to clear the air. I was concerned that he might end up as my guide on the summit attempt of Everest, and I sure didn't want to get into more conflict with him, especially considering how important it was to keep my head straight and focused on the tasks at hand instead of worrying about how he might continue to needle and shame me.

We met in the lobby of Hotel Yak and Yeti, an oasis of luxury after what we'd been through the past few months. There was endless hot water, actual heat in the rooms, and restaurants where I could order anything I wanted.

Marvin and I sat across from one another and there was definitely an uneasy silence between us. I decided to be as gracious and accommodating as I could with him, not wanting to trigger any additional tension between us.

"So," I began tentatively, "I know we had some difficulties on the mountain. I thought it might be a good idea for us to. . ."

Marvin kind of waved his hand, as if to say it was no big deal. I could see he was really uncomfortable with our situation when I was just trying to normalize things between us.

"Um, I was saying that I really value your help and expertise and the ways you try to support me." Okay, that was a stretch, if not a big fat lie, but as I said, I was just trying to deescalate any further problems between us. I was at a point where I sincerely believed I could handle the physical demands of the next level, but I was more concerned with what had felt like psychological torture. I'm not saying that's what Marvin intended, but rather that's what it had felt like to me.

Marvin just nodded noncommittally. I suppose he was wondering where I was going with this conversation and perhaps even thinking that I was still really upset and might get him in trouble or something. I needed to reassure him that was not at all what I intended.

"On Cho Oyu, you gave me a number of suggestions to improve my climbing and roping techniques, so I was wondering as I continue to prepare for Everest what other recommendations you might have for me?" As I said these words I thought to myself, "And please don't mention one more time those stupid water bottles!"

I could see visible signs of relief in Marvin's face once he realized that I wasn't there to argue with him but rather to try and be friends. We spent a pleasant hour chatting about some of the more amusing events that had transpired during our adventures, after which Marvin turned serious and once again repeated what he had told me toward the end of the climb when he admitted that I was a lot stronger and more resilient than he'd ever given me credit for. He actually said he was quite proud of me. I appreciated his graciousness in admitting he'd been wrong.

It was surprising that we'd actually reached a point in our relationship where Marvin told me he hoped he would be my guide on Everest, which was quite a turnaround. He also made some helpful suggestions about adjustments I could make to some of my equipment, including trying out a smaller size backpack that would better fit my smaller frame. We embraced in an awkward hug and promised to stay in touch.

Even though I was preparing to head home, I knew I'd be back in just a few more months with Jeffrey and some of his graduate students to spend time with the girls, a few of whom I'd met for the first time during this trip. It was, in fact, just two months later, barely recovered from my grueling Chinese expedition, that I returned to Kathmandu with my husband, Matt, and my aunt, to join Jeffrey's group to conduct the annual home and school visits. I was so excited to finally be able to show Matt my new world and all my new friends.

CHAPTER 12

— ⚘ —

Jeffrey: View of Everest

December, 2014 – January, 2015

MANY YEARS AGO, I developed a rather unique strategy for both raising money, as well as mentoring the children we support. I was well aware that throwing money at causes hardly makes much of a difference, especially in places where corruption and fraud are so rampant. Something like 90% of all charities in Nepal never distribute a single dollar to a cause; they just collect donations, pay themselves salaries and expenses so that there is little money left to distribute.

Empower Nepali Girls was constructed on a model of being completely transparent. Everyone pays their own expenses to visit Nepal. There were no salaried employees, not even an office until the last few years. Because I work with graduate students in counseling, many of them have been active in raising funds, but also traveling with me to Nepal to help mentor the girls.

Sara was excited to join our annual trip to distribute scholarships and visit all the children in the villages. I was in the process of transferring leadership to a new team that was headed by a former executive with eBay. I was also interested in recruiting Sara to take on a more active role within the organization because of her commitment and spectacular success raising money for the girls. On this particular trip, we had recruited 20 volunteers who had all been active in fundraising throughout the year. Some of those who were joining us had been involved for many years.

Our new president, Sameer, and his wife, Nikkole, were joining the trip, as well as several other veterans including Patrice, a professor at another university, and her family who had joined us before, and Sari, a psychiatrist, who arrived with her daughter, Emily. In addition to these experienced members, I invited along several of my graduate students, Kim, Heather, Karla, and Chelsea, all of whom had just completed their first semester in our counseling program. Each of them made a leap of faith to sign up even though they were already in debt supporting their studies. It seemed that almost everyone who joined these expeditions made huge sacrifices to do so, not only financially, but also choosing to be away from their loved ones during the Christmas/Chanukah and New Year's holidays.

My wife, Ellen, was joining us as well. She served as the foundation's bookkeeper and was returning to Nepal for perhaps the sixth time. Sara's husband, Matt, was also going to stay with us for part of the time because of his work schedule. He wanted to see this magical place that called to me so strongly. Finally, Ellen's cousin, Nancy, another tech executive, was the last part of our team. In addition, we had a small film crew with us who were creating a film production to showcase the work that the foundation was doing. The producer, Erin Galey, was especially interested in our work because she had just completed a feature film about sex trafficking in Nepal called *Brave Girl.*

Because our group was so large, we divided into smaller units to conduct the home and school visits. It was hardly feasible to show up to a girl's home the size of a small room, and file inside with two dozen people. The plan was for us to split in half throughout the visit, sending one group to one region while the others visited another area. Because we had so much territory to cover, more than a dozen villages spread across the country, this would allow us to visit almost every one of the 300 girls in the program.

Career Conference

One of the challenges we faced in the past was that our girls knew very little about the options available to them. They'd rarely ever seen a woman working in a profession. The only jobs they'd imagined for women were that of a teacher or a nurse. During the previous years we'd been trying to inspire them to strive for higher education and other career opportunities. When we asked them what they wanted to do when they got older, they'd always say a doctor, which was pretty unrealistic. There are so few spots available for any girls to go to medical school, no matter how smart they were. In many cases they weren't able to study math and science so we organized special tutoring for the few girls who had the highest school achievement records and would be most likely to be accepted into medical school.

It had been my original dream, fifteen years ago, that perhaps some-day our girls might become doctors and the next generation of leaders in their country. There were now two girls, Radha and Seema, who we'd been supporting for many years, and were now in the process of applying for medical school. Unfortunately, because they were from poor families, and had no connections with government officials; they were closed out of spots within Nepal, so we were arranging for them to study in Bangladesh. But, Many of our other girls also aspired to become doctors. This year our plan was to organize a career conference, as we'd done the prior year, to introduce them to possibilities they hadn't considered. We invited promi-nent Nepali women professionals to talk to the girls about their career paths.

We organized the event inside a school and it was packed with more than 150 of our girls, both from the Kathmandu Valley as well as those from outlying districts. These were children who lived in isolated, rural areas and had never even traveled on a bus before. Also, the day before, we had organized walking tours of all the famous temples and tourist sites so that both the girls and our U.S. volunteers would have the chance to get to know one another. The key to our mentoring program was for our team members to become role models for our girls since most of them were successful professionals. It was so intriguing for them to talk to Sara, who is an engineering professor, Sari who is a psychiatrist, Patrice who is a psy-chologist, Ellen who is an education professor, Nancy and Nikkole who are both technology executives, Emily who is beginning her university stud-ies, Erin who is a professional photographer, plus all my female graduate students pursuing their own ambitious careers. The girls never imagined it was possible that women would ever be allowed to do this kind of work.

Perhaps most impressive of all to them was Babita, our second in command after Pasang, who we had sponsored to complete her master's degree in social work. Because Pasang was busy so much of the time with his guiding responsibilities and executive functions of the organization, Babita takes care of most of the daily operations. And she is the one the girls go to when they need help. She is truly the prefect image of what we hoped for all our girls, to become contributing members to their communities.

We had invited Nepali women representing other professions to the conference, providing them with time to speak to the girls and tell their stories. We wanted to expose the girls to a variety of other careers for consideration that were not only more realistic, but also more affordable, given our limited budget and the astronomical costs of sponsoring girls in higher education, several thousand dollars for each girl per year instead of less than a hundred dollars.

The highlight of the conference was the viewing of Erin's new film that told the story of a 14-year-old Nepali girl who was tricked into leaving her village to find a good job in the city. Like many other such girls, she ended up being sold to a brothel in India. Erin thought it was fitting to premiere the movie, not at one of the major film festivals (that would soon follow) but for the very children she was hoping to help save.

Each year we sponsor a career conference in one of the regions of the country, transporting most of our 300 scholarship girls to that locale in order to learn more about professional opportunities from successful women who have achieved their goals. It is also an opportunity for our volunteers and team members to play games and interact informally with the children.

If you know anything about typical Bollywood films that are prevalent in this part of the world, the basic plot involves a love story (with lots of dancing and music) that always has a happy ending. The children gasped as the final scene in *Brave Girl* drew to a close because they'd never seen a film that ends with the protagonist ending up a sex slave, sentenced to die of repeated rape. We had hoped this would scare the heck out of them and show them the importance of being cautious and mistrusting of offers from strange men that sounded too good to be true. The film did its job for sure!

Afterwards, the main actress, Albina, who was still in high school herself and the same age as many of our older girls, spoke to the assembly not only about her experience making the film, but also about the extent that Nepali girls were being exploited, forced into early marriage, and sold into slavery. It was an incredibly powerful experience for all of us.

The Family Business

Empower Nepali Girls was always a kind of family business of sorts, with my wife, Ellen, taking care of financial issues; my son Cary, a lawyer, serving as the original legal counsel; and my friends, colleagues, and students filling more of our volunteer positions. Our dining room table served as headquarters since the inception of the organization because we didn't want to waste any money on office expenses.

It was a similar experience on the Nepal side of our operations. Pasang had converted several rooms in his house as the headquarters for our operation. He also recruited his whole family and many of his friends to become involved in our work. His wife hosts our gatherings and cooks meals for many events. His sister, a radio commentator, usually serves as our main speaker at ceremonies and conferences. His daughter, Chhusang, mentioned earlier as my assistant during the earthquake relief team, assists Babita with a variety of tasks. And so it goes that we have become one huge, blended family across the world. And I could see that

Sara was absolutely astounded by how personal and loving everyone was toward one another.

I know that one personal highlight for Sara was finally meeting Sonisha, the girl emblazoned on one of our posters that Sara had placed atop Cho Oyu and hoped to repeat again on the summit of Everest. Sonisha was now a beautiful woman of 20 attending business school to achieve her dream of becoming a banker. This is an unprecedented accomplishment for a girl who grew up in an isolated village near the Indian border. I had always been worried about her because she was so pretty and potentially vulnerable to exploitation, kidnapping, or being forced to marry. When Sara finally met Sonisha, she proudly showed her the photo on top of the mountain; it was like they'd known each other for years.

There were whispers among all our girls who realized that Sara was the woman who would be climbing Everest on their behalf. They looked at this relatively tiny, gorgeous woman, who is also an engineer! And they wondered how she could climb mountains on top of everything else she was doing in her career. They heard about her climb of Cho Oyu. But it wasn't those accomplishments that had impressed them as much as her accessibility. At any given moment there were several girls climbing on her lap, another holding on to her neck in one hug-ball of tickles and giggles. Whereas some of our team members were rather reluctant and, frankly frightened, by the strange environment with all the chaos around us, that didn't hold Sara back at all. She just dove into the crowd of children, asking them questions, hugging them, organizing games for them to play together.

"Mero nam Sara ho," she said to one group of girls, telling them her name in Nepali and they loved it, offering other words for her to pronounce, *sahti* (friend), *didi* (older sister), *dai* (older brother). After each repetition, they would carefully correct Sara's accent, absolutely loving the idea they could teach her their language. Then they tested her by telling Sara their names and asking her to go around the circle and repeat each of them in order.

My students observed her interactions curiously and then followed her lead, spreading out among the children to engage them. It was just one huge, sisterly gathering with little circles spread around the cavernous room or on the field outside the school, each of our volunteers engaged in various activities. Babita, and several of her friends and social work students, circulated among the crowd providing support as needed.

After the event was completed, all of us returned to Pasang's home to debrief, eat a traditional Nepali dinner of *dal baht*, drink and dance all night. I was so exhausted and jetlagged, I was on the verge of passing out, but Sara was out there dancing with all the other young women, imitating their traditional moves, and teaching them a few of her own. I had no idea where she had gotten that kind of energy, but it was obvious she had recovered physically from her last climb.

School Visits

The schedule and routines of these visits were structured around several main goals. The first priority was to make sure each of the girls was safe and well-supported and that our limited funds were being used wisely and most advantageously. Secondly, we usually conducted home visits, not just to see the children, but also to make sure that the families and parents understood clearly their own responsibilities to make sure their kids had time to devote to their school work. Thirdly, we conducted ceremonies to award the scholarships in public venues, both to honor the girls, as well as to demonstrate to their communities that we were around for the long haul. The challenge of this plan was that the schools and their villages were often located in very remote places, so it took a long time to make the circuit.

Bhaktapur was once the original capital of one of the kingdoms of Nepal. Although it would be devastated by the earthquakes a few months after this particular visit, it was one of my absolute favorite places in Nepal. Located just an hour from Kathmandu, it still looks like a medieval village with narrow, brick streets and people pretty much living as they have for thousands of years. It feels very much like taking a step back a millennium in time.

Dozens of our scholarship girls attend a school nearby so our team made their way to visit with the teachers, principal, and students. One of our concerns has always been that because our scholarship girls receive special attention and support, others would become envious, jealous, or otherwise sabotage or undermine our efforts. In order to counteract these feelings, we allot a limited budget for each school that our girls attend to provide some resources that are needed, whether computers, a printer, sports equipment, school supplies, or teaching materials. Once everyone is assembled, we distribute new backpacks and school supplies to our girls, and then provide the gifts to the school. This is usually followed by a celebration: tea and cookies, and then a traditional dance put on by the children.

One of the most enjoyable parts of the visits is that we assign each of our team members to visit classrooms and interact with the children who go absolutely crazy when one of us would step into the room. We teach them songs, and invite them to share their own. For some peculiar reason that I've never been able to figure out, as soon as I tell the children I'm from California, they start singing the Eagles song, "Hotel California!" I still have no idea how or why that particular tune has so embedded itself in their culture. We asked them questions in English so they could practice saying their names, telling us their favorite subjects, and who was in their families. If this makes it sound as if this was a relatively calm and organized affair in the classrooms, I haven't been clear enough—the kids were screaming, yelling for attention, jumping up and down, and the teachers looked on helplessly. It was obvious that these schools never had such exotic visitors from so far away. Sara and my students were especially a big hit because they are Asian, Latina, or Middle Eastern in origin, with black hair and eyes, and brown skin, very much resembling the Nepalis in appearance. The girls loved that especially, that women who look like them were doing such important things in their lives. It showed them that it may be possible for them, as well, to break out of the restricted mold for girls in their culture.

Each year we conduct a scholarship ceremony in the villages where our children reside, honoring them in front of their families and neighbors. We also provide them with school uniforms, shoes, warm jackets and hats, school supplies, books, tutoring, and pay their annual school fees. This can cost anywhere from about $75 per year to more than $3,000, depending on the age of the girl, the school she is attending, the location, and her field of study.

A Grand Time

After spending a week visiting with many of our children from the southern districts, as well as those within the Kathmandu Valley, we then split our team in half to visit the girls who live deep in the Everest and the Annapurna Himalayan regions. Although I'd flown to Lukla, the gateway to Sherpa culture, many times before, this would be Sara's first trip to finally see where she and her climbing team would be arriving a few months later. It was kind of an advanced scouting mission for her, as well as an opportunity to show Matt what things were like here.

It's remarkable to land a small plane in such a remote strip, sandwiched between high mountains in all directions, disembark and then to begin walking in one of the most beautiful places in the world. Our first stop, after fortifying ourselves with cappuccinos at the "fake" Starbucks (complete with a counterfeit green sign), was to visit the local school where several of our children attended. They had organized a ceremony and dance for us to celebrate the scholarship awards. As we sat together on the school's grounds, overlooking the Everest trail, we could see teams of climbers and trekkers passing by below us, so lost in their determined mission to reach Base Camp that they were oblivious to the people whose lives they were passing through.

Normally it would just be a two-hour walk to our lodge for the evening, but with frequent stops along the way to visit our girls in their homes, or talking to them along the trail, it took most of the day. Pasang had called ahead so everywhere we walked, children literally appeared out of nowhere to greet us, welcome us, and follow us along on our journey.

Our accommodations for the next few days would be at a meditation and retreat lodge that had been built by Pasang's cousin, Nima, who lived just across the river from Pasang's parent's home. Nima had spent many years living and working in Seattle, but he returned to his ancestral land in order to focus more on his meditation practice and to guide others in their own spiritual journeys. It was a huge structure that Nima's wife had designed, an architect who was now living in the U.S. full time. There was plenty of room for each of us, with a large central room with a wood-burning stove where we could host all the girls who live in the area.

The next day, prior to beginning our work, we took off for an acclimatization hike to help us adjust to altitude since eventually we would be going above 17,000 feet on this trip. This was perhaps not very high by Sara's standards, but for the rest of the group it was a lofty goal. We started up the mountain at dawn, a steep, narrow yak trail that weaved in and out through the forest until we reached a plateau with gorgeous views of the valley below. Everyone but Sara was exhausted and wanted to turn back, so we headed down knowing that a bunch of our girls were waiting for us at the lodge.

The children in this area tend to be extremely shy and the quality of the education is so poor that their English is sometimes a struggle to understand. The schools typically consist of stone buildings that might hold a handful of small rooms crowded with ancient wooden desks. Considering that it is absolutely freezing during winter months at this altitude above 10,000 feet, and some of the children don't have shoes, much less warm clothes, classes are cancelled until things warm up in the early spring.

We often organized our own impromptu classes for the children, helping them to practice their English and reviewing their math homework. I think what is most appreciated is that we feed them because many of them look like they've not had a good meal in a long time. While I was observing the interactions among our team members and several girls using iPads (which they'd never seen before) to teach them vocabulary, I heard screaming outside. I looked out the window to see Sara standing in the middle of a circle of about 20 girls. I wasn't sure what the rules of this game were all about, but by the sounds of their laughing and screams, they were all having a grand time.

Located high up on a ridge, overlooking the river valley below, was another school that served children who were still more isolated. There were steep cliffs that seemed to precariously balance their homes. I remember one of our scholarship girls and her family died the previous year when a mudslide washed them away. She was an adorable little girl who I once held on my lap and it still saddens me to think about her.

Each school we visited had their own special ceremony to honor us as important, foreign visitors. In one particular place we watched more than 200 children doing their morning warmup exercises. This was followed by dancing which was joined by several among our group, moving gracefully as they lined up behind the children. Then Sara got up in front to demonstrate Persian dances, which absolutely delighted the children who followed every step and move.

Breakfast with Everest

We continued onward and upward through villages, sometimes following the standard trekking route, but more often than not following yak trails along the ridges where many of our children lived way off the beaten trail. During each home visit we would be offered tea, or sometimes little boiled potatoes (about all that they could harvest and store this time of year). We would sit and visit for several minutes and then ask each girl to show us her schoolwork. Before leaving and moving on to the next place, we would take turns speaking to the parents and urging them to support their girl's study. It was exhausting and emotionally draining,, seeing how these people lived. There were times when I would hear their stories of hardship and deprivation and I could barely hold in my own anguish before I would walk outside and start sobbing uncontrollably. Even though I'm a psychologist by profession, and I'd been visiting the children for so many years, I still couldn't deal with all the suffering. There were times when each of us would take turns comforting one another as we'd lose control.

It was frankly with some relief that we completed our last school and home visits and now had a full week to do some trekking in this beautiful area. This was intended both as a reward and also as sacred reflective time to metabolize all we'd seen and done. It was also useful for us to process everything together, debrief about what seemed to work best, and make future plans for what needed to be done next. It was Pasang's idea, for instance, that some of the more talented girls might be brought to Kathmandu in order to receive a better education. There was one girl, only 10 years old, who had performed a dance recital for us and was so remarkably talented that she had already placed second in the nation for her age group. We thought it might be a good idea to hire a professional choreographer for her to further improve her performances since this might become a viable career. She'd already been invited to Korea for a performance.

The next few days were so wonderfully relaxing—and vigorous. This was nothing like Sara's summit attempts, but it was still pretty challenging terrain as we moved up higher and higher, and the weather got colder and colder. We were headed toward Namche Bazaar, the capital of the Sherpa Empire, but rather than going into the village itself, which I'd done a half-dozen times previously, our goal was a lodge perched high on a 15,000-foot mountain that overlooked the village below. This would be the highest that any of us had slept previously.

Enjoying breakfast while watching the sun rise over Mt. Everest, the dark, triangular mountain in the middle, rising above the ridge.

The next day we climbed a mountain topping off at over 17,000 feet. It took most of the day because of the deep snow. By the time we returned to the lodge, everyone immediately headed to bed, everyone except Sara who decided she wanted to do the climb a second time; after all, she was now training for Everest.

The morning of our departure, breakfast was set out for us in the most elegant setting imaginable. There was a dining table and chairs, each emblazoned with ribbons and bows, positioned toward Mount Everest rising in the distance. This was the best view Sara had yet of her next destination. With complete reverence we watched the sun rise above the Himalayas, bathing the majestic mountain in pink light. Afterwards we would begin the long, arduous walk back down the mountain, through all the villages, past all our girls standing along the trail, to the airport in Lukla, to Kathmandu, and then home. We never realized that everything in this area of the country, in this region of the world, particularly where we were sitting, would be leveled by the earthquakes that would soon follow.

CHAPTER 13

———— ⚬ ————

Sara: Finally Ready for Everest

February - March, 2015

MY MEMORIES OF the follow-up trip back to the Everest region that Jeffrey described in the preceding chapter were so special and unlike anything I've experienced, much less imagined. It was incredible to have Matt with me, as well as my aunt, and several of Jeffrey's graduate students, to be able to show them this beautiful country and these amazing people.

As I was beginning my final preparations and training for my third trip to Nepal during the same year, I couldn't help but draw even more motivation and strength from my memories of the children that continued to haunt me. I remembered, in particular, visiting one classroom in which I asked the girls to come up to the front so I could test them on their favorite subjects. If they'd say math, then I'd write a quadratic equation on the board and ask them to solve it, thinking there'd be no way they'd have such an advanced grasp of these concepts. And if they'd say science, then I'd pose a difficult question about biology or chemistry. But what shocked me was even with their minimal resources, no equipment, and only a few books to share, these girls were absolutely brilliant.

I recall visiting one girl's home so she could show me her homework. While I sat on a straw stool by the fire and sipped chai tea, Priti went into the back to retrieve a notebook. I noticed that half the pages were devoted to chemistry, and the other half to English grammar. "Why are you using one notebook for both subjects?" I asked her.

Priti kind of shrugged. "I only have this one notebook."

When I heard that, I could feel tears beginning to form, and I realized I was not only crying for this smart girl who wanted so badly to do well in school, but also crying for myself when I remembered that I, too, couldn't afford notebooks when I started university at UCLA—until that magical truck came by.

I pretended the smoke was making my eyes water and wiped them with my sleeve. "So," I said in a shaky voice, "show me what you are doing in science," and she proceeded to turn the pages and point out what she'd been learning.

"Okay," I said after a long pause, "if you mix sulfuric acid with calcium, write out the equation for me to show the result."

Priti broke out in a huge grin, not at all shy any longer, and immediately wrote it out.

"Wow," I said, genuinely impressed. "So, what do you intend to do with all this science?"

She mumbled something, retreating back into shyness once again.

"What's that you said? Speak up!"

"I said a doctor. I want to be a doctor." She was almost embarrassed to say this out loud because it seemed like such a ridiculous fantasy.

"Good for you!" I said, grabbing her shoulders and giving her an affectionate hug. "You are so, so smart. You can do this! And I can help you." In that moment, I not only felt I would climb Everest, but I'd be willing to climb all the way to the moon so that Priti, and the other girls like her, could pursue their dreams.

Training Flashbacks

In order to take things to the next level of my training, I hired a coach, Tim, who specialized in preparing elite athletes and mountaineers. The first thing Tim told me was quite surprising in that he said most of the work we'd be doing together would be inside my head rather than merely strengthening my muscles and conditioning my endurance. He warned me that he would push me so far beyond my limits that I would no longer be certain how far I could really go. After all, so much of climbing is mental stamina, being able to tolerate discomfort and suffering. And he explained that this training would not only improve my performance on the mountain but in all other aspects of my life.

I knew exactly what Tim meant because based on my experiences already in the mountains, I realized I was a very different person than I used to be, so much more tolerant and patient. I also felt like there was almost nothing that was beyond my reach. After all, if someone like me with no experience, no previous training—or even exposure—to climbing, could scale some of the highest peaks in the world, surely almost anything else was possible. These were the kinds of thoughts I repeated to myself over and over when Tim devised new and ingenious ways to push me beyond my limits during our daily sessions.

Pretty early in our program, Tim greeted me at the gym with a grin on his face that he could barely restrain. "I've got a special treat for you today."

Training for Everest involved rigorous, brutal exercises on a daily basis to increase my strength and stamina, but much of the work also involved preparing my mind for the life-threatening challenges I would face.

"Oh yeah?" I answered with some trepidation, wondering what he could possibly have dreamed up next after we had already run through the usual assortment of boot camp exercises.

"Voila!" Tim said, and pointed over his shoulder at a contraption that looked like a medieval torture device: it was actually a sled with weights on it, attached to long ropes.

I looked at it quizzically, and he explained with a laugh that this was my new "friend."

Tim connected me to the device, sat on the sideline with a bottle of vitamin water, and then proceeded to scream at me to pull the thing back and forth across the room. Every time I lagged a little, he would rise up and follow me, yelling at me to go faster.

Sweat was dripping down my back. I could barely catch a breath. This was insane. This was just out of control. I couldn't do this. I knew that I was supposed to stay focused on the task at hand, not try to run away from the pain in my head and instead stay with it. It had been explained to me that one thing that separates world class athletes from amateurs or underachieving pros is that the best among them stay with their suffering rather than try to escape from it. Instead of lapsing into fantasy, distracting themselves with music or podcasts, or trying to anesthetize the pain, really great athletes embrace their suffering. They concentrate even harder on their breathing, their foot placement, their technique. They use the pain as valuable input regarding how far, and how hard, they can push themselves without falling apart.

Nevertheless, I found continued solace and comfort during my brutal training sessions by thinking about the girls I was doing all of this for. I had the most vivid flashbacks and the most intense flooding of memories at unpredictable times. All of a sudden I could remember being back in Nepal, and the sled I was pulling, or the wall I was climbing, would just disappear and I would feel this perfect sense of calmness.

On this particular day, when I was first introduced to the sled, it was like I went into a trance and I was transported back to one teahouse we visited where there were a few dozen of our scholarship girls assembled.

We started dancing with the girls. The little ones were so light that I could hold two little kids at the same time and dance with them, pick them up, put them down. I tried to remember games from my own childhood that we could play together but they insisted they wanted to teach me and Jeffrey one of their favorite activities that they called "Cat and Rat." They invited Jeffrey and me into the center of a huge circle with all the girls holding hands around us. They blindfolded each of us and explained that I would be the rat and I was supposed to make a rat-like sound, "Chee chee, Chee chee," and that Jeffrey was supposed to try and catch me, signaling his whereabouts calling out, "Meow meow." Of course we were both blind so it was pretty hilarious for the kids to watch Jeffrey trying to catch me, who apparently was doing all kinds of crazy things, slithering on the ground, exaggerating his movements with feline grace, all the while the children were screaming their heads off.

I was momentarily jolted back to the present when I heard Tim speaking to me in a soft voice I could barely hear because I had tuned him out while I was lost in the past. "That's enough," he repeated again, telling me it was time for a well-deserved rest.

This was to be my routine for the next few months: going to the gym during the day, running up and down mountains at night, taking care of all the hundreds of details to replace some equipment, and put my life in order for the months I would once again be gone.

A Moment I'll Never Forget

If I was inexperienced as a mountain climber, I was just as clueless when it came to my main job related to this endeavor, which was to raise money to support the children. After all, that's the reason I was doing all this. I tried to get my friends involved as much as possible, as they have an assortment of skills that are beyond me. We put together several fundraising events, with very limited success since most of the people I knew had already made donations and others within the Persian community preferred to target charities that focused exclusively on Iran.

Logistics for our upcoming trip were coming together. I received a message introducing everyone who would be on our team and I learned two important pieces of information. First, that Marvin would not be joining us because he was leading another expedition, which was quite a relief. And secondly, that my tent mate would be a woman who was an accomplished climber with lots of experience in the Himalayas. I learned that Kate was not only the chief finance officer of a company but also the mother of four children. I reasoned she must be even more incredible to be able to take care of all those people and yet still negotiate a way to escape for several months while the company and her family ran themselves. I was imagining how great it would be to introduce Kate to our girls so they could see a strong woman who not only has an important job, but also she also takes care of her family and *still* finds time to pursue her own interests.

I remembered during the last trip when we first landed in Lukla with Matt and Jeffrey's group as soon as we crawled out of the small plane, we immediately hiked a few minutes up to a school to meet all the children there. I was picturing someone like Kate joining us and how I could show her and all the others around and have them meet the kids and their parents. There was one girl, Sarmila, who had to walk several hours to school every day because her home was so far away from the village. On the particular day we arrived, school was closed because of the freezing temperatures, but many of the girls came to the school to meet us anyway.

Afterwards, we went to visit the homes of the some of the girls and I had tried to remember the routes to get there so I could return when I came with my Everest team. There was one home, more like a little hut, that could barely hold more than a few people. There were dirt floors and the walls were made of mud and stone. The door was just a blanket draped across the entrance. Our scholarship girl was living with her grandparents since the father had abandoned the family long ago.

Once we all settled ourselves inside, elbow to elbow, Jeffrey told the grandfather how proud he must feel that his granddaughter was so smart and was doing so well in school. I spoke up as well and mentioned that I'd be coming back to check on her with my friends in a few months when I was on my way to climb Everest.

The grandfather's eyes lit up and he nodded. "Right now," he said, "I am happier than the summit of Mt. Everest."

It was a moment I'll never forget, and one that continues to inspire me. I just kept picturing what it would be like to sit here with them a few months from now, and wondering what my teammates will think of all this.

Hanging out with many of our scholarship recipients in the Everest region.

Final Departure

After all these months, even years of planning, the time had finally come for me to say farewell and begin the final steps of this journey. Matt drove me to the airport and the whole way he kept telling me how proud he was of me and what I was doing. You can't imagine how much that meant to me, especially considering the guilt I felt leaving him behind for a few months. The one thing we didn't speak about was the very real possibility I would never be coming home again.

All my friends and family had surprised me by showing up at the airport to wish me a safe journey. They were wearing tee-shirts with my photo on it, and the words, "Go, Sara, you can do it!" They had made signs displaying their love and support. My best friend, Pari, had written a letter that she handed me, saying, "Read this when you need to be stronger." Then we embraced and both started crying.

So many others solemnly gave me bon voyage gifts, a stuffed animal, a bag of dried fruit, a warm scarf, a few lemons (my favorite food). Matt's cousin, Mo, handed me a bag of In-N-Out burgers, which is somewhat of a cult food in this part of the country. "I know you're gonna miss these for sure," he said.

Once settled on the plane, I checked for messages one last time and found my inbox stuffed with good tidings. There was an email from Jeffrey saying, "You are the strongest person that I know," and it meant a lot to me knowing how strong he himself is, and how many people he knows in the world. I had emails from my neighbors, from Matt's childhood friends, as well as several from my friends who I hadn't heard from in years, and I wondered how they even knew about what I was doing. I was overwhelmed with this much love and I started to feel terribly guilty because I knew there was a chance that I was not only putting my own life in jeopardy, but also the welfare of so many others who would also suffer as a result. My constant reassurance was the reminder that this trip wasn't about me at all; it was for the girls.

Once the plane took off, I just stared out the window for hours, wondering if this was the last time I'd ever see the Pacific Ocean. I was trying to be realistic that no matter how careful I was on the mountain, there were so many things that could go wrong that were out of my control—the weather, unstable ice, an unmarked crevasse, a mistake by a climber in front of me. Of course it never occurred to me that an earthquake could be a factor, especially one that would bring the whole mountain down on top of us.

Blessings

When I arrived back at the hotel in Kathmandu, I immediately recognized many of our Sherpas from Cho Oyu, including Lakpa, hanging out in the lobby. It was interesting, though, that they didn't recognize me! I had since cut off most of my hair, thinking it would make things so much easier for me on the mountain since I had so few opportunities to wash it.

As I approached the group, I could finally see some looks of recognition, from Lakpa first, and then Eric, our lead guide. I was pretty damn excited that Eric would be in charge of our team. He was one of the most experienced and accomplished climbers anywhere, having summited Kilimanjaro 65 times, Denali 13 times, as well as many of the Himalayan peaks. But just as important to me, he was kind, patient, and accessible. I'd have no fear whatsoever that he would ever publically (or even privately) humiliate me. In addition to Eric and Lakpa, we'd have Damian with us, an Argentinian who had summited Everest five times previously.

I had arrived before any of the others on our team because I wanted to have some time to visit with our girls and see Babita, Pasang, and his family. I asked Eric to check my gear for me to make sure everything was in order and then I took off for the day with Babita, who picked me up on her motor scooter so we could hang out at Pasang's house. They had prepared a special Nepali dinner for me with *momos* (dumplings), *dal baht* (rice and lentils), and a cake for dessert that said, "Good luck, Sara" on the icing. Then all the girls from the area started streaming in to show their respect and appreciation, offering me gifts and notes and cards. The littlest girls had drawn pictures for me and they all insisted I bring their messages with me on the mountain. The girls presented me with flowers and placed *khatas* around my neck, silk scarves blessed by the Dalai Lama.

I had never felt as blessed as I did in that moment. All these people and children showed up to honor and thank me for what I was doing on their behalf. They held a celebration in my honor and we all danced together, singing songs and holding hands. There were never fewer than three little girls squirming on my lap at any one time. It was just a magical evening, but I was so totally wasted after no sleep and jetlag that I was ready to go back to the hotel and meet the rest of my team.

Just as I was getting ready to leave, an older lady approached me. She was tiny, rail thin, and appeared even smaller because she was hunched over and could barely shuffle along. She reached out her hands to hold my own and started talking to me in Nepali, in a soft voice that I could barely hear, much less understand the words. Babita came over to help translate.

"I am grandmother," the woman said to introduce herself to me.

"Namaskar," I replied, bowing and holding my hands level with my face, rather than below my chin, to show respect for an elder. With someone older, it is the custom to show even more respect by holding one's hands higher and using the honorific form of "Namaste."

"She is my granddaughter," the woman said, pointing to one of the girls I'd been dancing with.

"Yes, she's beautiful."

"She does not have parents. I am the only one."

I just nodded, not sure if that meant she was an orphan, or that her parents had died, or perhaps had even abandoned the little girl.

"I am sick," the woman said. "I have the cancer. I will not live much longer."

I looked toward Babita who was translating the conversation. I wasn't sure what to say or what to do. This was just breaking my heart.

"Can you help us?" the woman asked me. "Can you help my granddaughter stay in school after I'm gone? Can you find others to care for her? She's very smart. And she likes to go to school. But now, I don't know what will happen to her when I'm not here."

What else could I possibly say to this woman except that of course I would help her granddaughter? I'd already heard so many stories like this with so many of our girls, and each one inspired me to redouble my efforts to help them. By gosh, I was going to get to the top of Everest if it killed me.

Meet the Team

By the time I returned to the hotel that evening, the rest of our team members had arrived and were getting settled. Orion was a banker by profession, a very tall guy who I immediately felt a connection to because of his warmth and kindness. Steve was also in the banking business from Canada and shared a lot of common values and interests with me. He had been supporting children in Afghanistan for many years and was the one who was most interested in the work we were doing with girls in Nepal. Then there was Jon, from Australia, a very gregarious, charming, and friendly fellow who turned out to be one of my absolute favorites. Because he was also an electrical engineer by training, we had a lot in common and would spend a lot of time deep in conversation during our journey. "Aussie Jon" had tried climbing Everest the previous year but had been turned back because of the avalanches that had killed so many people. The same thing had happened with Tom, from Portland, a lawyer who was back to try again this year. The final member of our team, Kate, who would be my tent mate, brought her 11-year-old son, Sean, along with a tutor to keep the schoolwork going while they waited at Base Camp when we were up in the mountains. I found it pretty remarkable that an 11-year-old Western kid could manage to trek up and down the steep mountains we would navigate on the Everest trail, which is pretty grueling in places.

I couldn't possibly have been any happier with our team, our leader, and our Sherpas. Everyone was so friendly and supportive, no big egos or overly demanding, entitled people, which surprised me considering how prominent and wealthy most Everest climbers tend to be. Sufficiently reassured after meeting everyone, I took my leave once again to return to the Rising Rays School that I had visited during my last trip to Nepal. There was the usual lineup of children waiting to greet me with flowers and *khatas*. They had made a big sign, wishing me luck on the expedition.

All the children crowded around me, peppering me with questions about the upcoming climb. They wanted to know how I trained for Everest and what it was like for a woman to do what men usually do. They wanted to know what I would eat on the mountain, where and how I would poop, whether I'd be using supplemental oxygen. They just found it so funny when I told them that it was so cold outside at night that I had to use a funnel to pee in a bottle.

Kumar, the principal of the school, was laughing right along with them and posed a few interesting questions himself about our plans for reaching the summit. I patiently answered each and every question because I wanted them to understand just how difficult and dangerous this journey would be, what was at stake, not only for me, but for them as well. I wanted them to know the hardships I would be facing. Then I had leverage to ask them to promise that their role in this partnership would be to continue to study hard and do their best in school.

The next day we flew back to Lukla and continued on to Phakding, the village just a few hours away where many of our girls live. Pasang had alerted the children that I'd be coming through there with our expedition, so I wasn't surprised to see the girls waiting for us along the side of the trail. Over the years they must have seen thousands of trekkers and climbers walk by them, as if they were just an invisible part of the scenery, but this time they knew they were waiting for a friend and guest who had promised to return to them, who had promised to support them.

I collected about 30 of the girls who had turned up and escorted them all back to the teahouse where we were staying so I could introduce them to my friends and climbing partners. Each one of the girls introduced herself, then proceeded to offer a *khata* to each of us, wishing us safe passage. Then the usual dancing and games began. This time it included Steve and Aussie Jon, Orion, Tom, Kate, Sean, and all the Sherpas. As many times as they'd been to this part of the world, they'd never seen or experienced anything quite like this, all the incredible energy in the room, and all the children's dreams that hung in the balance of whether support for them would continue. Many of these people have since become our most loyal and dependable donors and are now among my closest friends.

We could only remain there for one night before we had to continue onward, so we hugged the girls to say goodbye. Many of them had walked

Our Everest expedition team, staying in a teahouse on the way to Base Camp.

three hours to greet us and now had to turn around and head back home before dark. We would continue up the trail during the next few days, and all along the way I would see some of our girls waving in their bright red puffy jackets, sometimes coming down the ridge to say hello and wish us good fortune.

They were long days on the trail on the way to Base Camp, occasionally stopping a few times to do some acclimatizing hikes. We were still getting used to one another's pace, learning about one another, trading stories about previous mishaps or adventures. Aussie Jon was pretty hilarious most of the time. The other guys were incredibly nice and supportive as well. But I found myself gravitating to Kate and her son, Sean, the most. Given that Matt and I had been talking about starting a family of our own pretty soon, after I got this climbing stuff out of my system, I was fascinated by the way that Kate managed to pursue her interests at the same time she was such a devoted mother. I so envied the relationship that she and Sean had and wondered if I'd be able to do that with my own son or daughter someday.

I'd been thinking about this very idea when Damian walked up next to me and scrutinized me with a searching look. I must have appeared lost in concentration, or looked worried, because he placed a hand on my arm to stop me for a moment. "I know you had some difficulties on Cho Oyu," he said to me. I think he was referring to the fact that I'm so much smaller than everyone else. "But you have a very strong mind. And that is more important than the body. If you listen to us, if you follow our directions and do the things we tell you, I think you can get to the summit of the highest place in the world."

CHAPTER 14

—— ❦ ——

Sara: Base Camp and Beyond

April, 2015

AFTER A COUPLE of days walking along the trail, we arrived in Namche Bazaar. It is a rather large village for this remote region, a trading and commercial center for both climbers and trekkers on their way to Base Camp, as well as local people who show up for the weekly markets. There are not only businesses with climbing equipment and supplies, but also bakeries and tourist shops.

As we entered the valley and began the steep climb up to the lodge where we'd be staying, I was walking alongside Aussie Jon who was always plying me with interesting questions about my life and work. He had been asking me about how to better encourage girls and women to go into engineering, a challenge that was not only the case in Nepal, but also elsewhere. Almost all of my technical students back home were men. As an engineer himself, he understood that whereas that profession is usually associated with building cars, planes, robots, and missiles, traditionally male-dominated interests, women tend to be focused on solving different problems related to health and well-being. Then Kate joined the conversation and we ended up talking about having children, which is a subject I found endlessly fascinating.

Conversations

From Namche, our next stop was Tengboche, a World Heritage site and the location of a monastery situated on top of a mountain with a hundred monks living there. The nature of the trail was that we were constantly going down to the glacial river, crossing rickety bridges suspended over the gorge, then climbing all the way back up to continue along the path. Since we had an extra acclimatizing day for recovery, we had scheduled an audience with the Lama, the head monk, in order to bless our journey.

All along the trek to Base Camp, from one village to the next, climbing higher and higher, we met and talked with other climbers along the way. I met one guy, who was with another alpine guiding company. He disclosed that he was almost completely inexperienced in high altitudes except for one climb in the Andes. I wondered what he, and his team, must be thinking to bring people up here who were so unprepared? It terrified me that there would be climbers like that on our ropes and ladders.

One of the most intriguing parts of these trips is not just the climbing but the opportunities to get to know such interesting people who attempt such adventures. Everyone has a great story to tell about why they are doing this, or what they do back in the world. I had been walking with Eric, our lead guide, for the previous hour as we were approaching the last stop before arriving at Base Camp. We had topped off at 17,000 feet at that point, so it helped to keep conversations going between deep breathing.

I asked him at one point, "How does your wife handle you being gone so much of the time?" I had been thinking about Matt and how often during the last years we'd been separated because of my climbs on Cho Oyu, Rainier, Aconcagua, and other mountain. I figured I had been gone more than six months during the past two years.

Eric shrugged. "It really is hard on relationships," he admitted. "A lot of people can't handle that, I suppose."

"So, how do you handle the guilt and all?"

Eric was a pretty wise fellow, who had obviously given these questions considerable thought, and had likely talked about this with a lot of other climbers. Still, he didn't have much of an answer other than this was just something he needed to do and he was lucky to have a partner who understood that. I realized that I was pretty fortunate, as well, that Matt was so supportive. But I also realized that at some point this stage of my life was going to end. It was then that I made a deliberate point to look around more carefully, to burn the views into my memory so I would never forget where I was, where I'd been, and where I was going next.

I've mentioned how sleeping at high altitude is always challenging. Even more disturbing, at times, are the strange dreams that occurred whenever I did manage to fall unconscious. They were so vivid and intense they were almost like hallucinations, so much so that sometimes I couldn't tell if they were real or not. I had one particularly powerful dream the night before we arrived at Base Camp in which all the members of our team spoke fluent Farsi. When I greeted everyone at breakfast the next morning, I started speaking to them in my native language until I realized that they couldn't understand me and thought I'd lost my mind.

That day we headed up, up, up to Lobuche, the site of a memorial to all the climbers who died on Everest. There was a huge brass plaque embedded in the rocks that read, "May he have accomplished his dreams."

As we stood there silently, offering prayers to the departed, I could feel myself holding back tears, as much for the dangers I was about to face as for all those who had perished. As I read the inscription, I also shook my head, thinking that, first of all, I didn't think dying was part of the dreams they hoped to accomplish and, secondly, I noted the masculine "he" as a reminder that besides me and Kate, there were not many other women climbers that we'd yet seen.

I felt this incredible pressure to show everyone, especially the men, that I could keep up with them. During these last few days it felt like I was an actor on a stage, pretending to be strong, relaxed, and fit. The truth was that I had an excruciating headache, felt dehydrated no matter how much water I drank (Marvin would have been pleased.), and I had no appetite. I just stood in front of this memorial and wondered, given how uncomfortable I already felt, whether I would end up being a part of this memorial. These morbid thoughts were interrupted by a wet tongue licking my hand. I looked down to find our new friend and dog companion who had been following us for the past week and was now our good luck

charm. We had named him Khumbu after the Icefall we could see looming in the distance.

I rolled my shoulders and tried to stretch out my back that was stiff
from carrying my big backpack. I felt like a mess already and we hadn't
even gotten close to the really hard part. So far we hadn't even done
much climbing at all during our acclimatizing hikes, just mostly going up
and down to get used the thin air and cold. That was about to change and
become a lot more challenging.

Base Camp

Whatever excitement I felt about finally arriving at Base Camp was tempered by the blizzard-like conditions outside. Even though we were staying in a teahouse, it had been so cold during the night that I had slept
with all my clothes on inside my sleeping bag with a hot water bottle
underneath my back. It had been a brutal night as I could hear everyone
snoring and moving around.

We got a late start so we ended up following "yak trains" carrying
supplies as well as other climbing teams. It was like a parade slowly making its way through the soft snow that was fast accumulating on the trail.
I was concentrating so hard on my foot placements that I was startled
to feel something hit my back. I looked over my shoulder to see another
group of climbers behind me, grinning and pointing at one another to
blame whoever had thrown the snowball. I couldn't just ignore this over-
ture so I hurried around the next turn in the trail to prepare an ambush.
With the poor visibility, hiding was pretty easy and I had my revenge. In
fact, a whole battle ensued among more than a dozen of us launching our
missiles, giggling, running around like crazy. For the first time in a while,
I finally felt warm.

Once we arrived at Base Camp I was shocked at how big the place
was. It was like a tent city with hundreds of brightly colored structures that
housed the headquarters and sleeping quarters for the dozens of teams
that were hoping to summit Everest. What surprised me most, however,

Often our acclimatizing and training climbs from Base Camp occurred under blizzard conditions, requiring us to stomp through deep snow at times.

was how many people I already knew who were there, climbers I'd not only met along the trail but also those I had encountered during previous expeditions in the Andes, Cascades, and Himalayas.

I was also pleased to see that we wouldn't exactly be deprived of many comforts and luxuries while settled at Base Camp. Our guides and porters had been sent ahead to erect a large tent that would serve as our headquarters and dining room. In addition, each of us had set up our own tents like circling a wagon train. There was a party atmosphere everywhere, with reggae music blaring, competing with Nepali songs and rock standards. Hundreds of climbers were going about their business, organizing their equipment, lounging around, making phone calls or sending messages back home, some leaving or returning from training climbs.

Meanwhile the snow was falling and was expected to continue for the next week, which was not good news at all for our prospects since there would be greater dangers of avalanches, hidden crevasses, deep snow, and unstable conditions. The "ice fall doctors," Sherpas who are responsible for setting up the ropes and installing the ladders across crevasses and up ice walls, were out in the snowstorm working their magic. We were told it would be a few more days before they would be completed.

My own tent was easy to find because I had attached an Empower Nepali Girls flag to the side, the same banner I intended to take with me up to the top. This became a beacon for others to approach me and ask about our organization and what we were doing. Before long, it was like the charity's headquarters with people asking how they could donate or support our cause. As I've mentioned, many of the climbers were wealthy and privileged, so perhaps they felt their own guilt that they were investing so much time, money, and energy for the sole purpose of transporting themselves to the top of a mountain. It was quite a fertile environment for me to spread the word about our mission, especially considering that the climbers had been seeing our girls, or many just like them, all along the journey.

There is always a settling in and adjustment to each of our temporary homes. Since we'd be staying in these tents, on and off, for the next two months, it was even more important to get everything set up properly. Although we only bring the stuff with us that we can carry on our own backs, and that fit into a single duffel bag carried by a porter, it always seemed like a challenge to find what you need when you decide you need it most. So the first thing I usually do is try to organize my equipment so I can find the things that are a priority. This time, however, I was sopping wet, through and through, from the blizzard and snowball fight, and I could feel the shivers start to take hold. I was also so tired I could barely open my duffel bag. I was just going to drag out my sleeping bag and try to get some rest when I heard a helicopter land nearby. I poked my head outside to see what was going on and learned that Sean, Kate's son, was being transported back to Kathmandu now that the climbing part of our expedition would begin.

Empower Nepali Girls headquarters at Everest Base Camp

At that point, sleep was out of the question so I decided to have a look around my new village, which struck me as a pretty wild and crazy place with lots of interesting characters. The first thing I learned was that we actually had Internet access in this remote place. I was able to communicate with people back home and tell them that I was in fine spirts and perfect health. Okay, so I lied a little.

There was actually a complete hospital setup in the camp so I walked by to check it out and found it fully stocked with medicine, equipment, and qualified physicians who specialized in high altitude medicine. I asked a few questions while I was there, and the staff reassured me that my own symptoms were perfectly normal and would eventually dissipate once I fully acclimatized. Of course, every time we went higher, my body would have to adapt all over again, at least until we reached a height where the body stops adapting altogether and starts dying from lack of oxygen.

There was another Puja ceremony scheduled, similar to what we'd done at Cho Oyu, in which we asked for blessing and safe passage on the mountain. Given that the year before, so many Sherpas had died and nobody was able to summit, this ritual took on special meaning. We rubbed flour on one another's faces and offered rice as a gift to the gods, blessing our crampons and ice axes. I had also brought along my Empower Nepali Girls banner to receive a blessing as well. Then with the prayers completed, we all started dancing, Khumbu the dog barking hysterically and jumping around along with us.

Once the festivities ended, I realized how sick I was actually feeling. In addition to the vice-like headache that was squeezing my brain, I had a sore throat and felt completely lethargic. It was an effort to even stroll back to my tent and rest. Kate, sweetheart that she was, stopped by to check on me and brought a glass of warm salt water to gargle with, hoping it would soothe my throat. Even Khumbu seemed to notice I wasn't quite right, so he stood vigil outside my tent where he lay down for his own nap.

When I awoke the next day, I felt much better, enough so that I could manage our scheduled acclimatizing hike up to Pumori Peak at 19,000 feet. In the Sherpa language, Pumori means "unmarried daughter" and it is often referred to as Everest's little daughter. Although it is not very technical or difficult compared to the "big father" next to it, close to 50 people have lost their lives in avalanches trying to get to the top. Of course we didn't know it at the time, but Pumori would be the source of the avalanche that would come crashing down a few weeks later during the earthquake and completely destroy Base Camp.

Thousand Island Dressing

After a rare decent night's rest, I was able to keep up with everyone during the climb, which was certainly reassuring given my altitude sickness. By comparison to Pumori, it felt relatively oxygen-rich back down at Base Camp, which was a good feeling. And when I saw my tent again, with the banner across it, I couldn't help but smile about being "home" again.

It was a remarkable luxury to be able to check email and Facebook through the Internet access. There was a message from Jeffrey waiting for me who I knew, along with Matt and others, was carefully tracking my progress. "How are you doing?" he wrote me. "How is your team? Do you like the team members? How are your guides? You might feel alone at times, but know that all of us, all your family, friends and all the girls, are cheering for you. So you're not alone. You're climbing with all of us with you."

After our long day, that was certainly reassuring, but there was one more gift waiting for me when I arrived at the dining room tent. As you might imagine, given that we burn up to 5,000 calories in a single day with all our strenuous exercise, food is really, really important—doubly so because altitude takes away your appetite and there really aren't that many foods that are all that appealing besides chocolate. In addition, there are limited meal choices in camp that usually alternate between stir-fried noodles and stir-fried rice. Even ketchup and the most basic condiments are coveted as a way to spice up the meals a little. I had put in a special request when I asked Lakpa some time ago to bring along Thousand Island dressing as an option to pour on top whatever mixture was set before us.

Once we sat down for our meal, Lakpa presented the bottle with a flourish and everyone applauded in excitement. Little did I realize we only had that one bottle and it was polished off pretty quickly. This concerned me because I had a secret plan to drench everything with the dressing to make it more palatable. If I couldn't consume enough food, I'd lose too much weight and wouldn't be able to climb. The guides would actually weigh us every few days and if we lost too many pounds, we'd get sent home.

Because of all the deaths in the Icefall the previous year, there were a lot of news media at Base Camp wanting to interview climbers regarding the anniversary of the 16 Sherpas who were buried in avalanches. The same questions come up every time there are tragedies like this: "Why are you risking your life, and the lives of so many local people, just to say you stood on top of Everest? What safeguards are you taking to protect your Nepali staff from accidental injuries or death?"

I wanted to get some publicity for our girls so I had to figure out a way to change the subject once the cameras were rolling. Orion decided that he'd be my manager and publicity consultant on this project, so we spent a lot of time strategizing ways that I could bring greater awareness to the plight of girls in Nepal. All along, Orion was my main cheerleader. He'd often walk behind me on our hikes and climbs, encouraging me the whole way when he could see me struggling. "You can do this," he'd whisper to me. "Take your time. One step at a time. We'll do this together."

There was special memorial ceremony held on April 18 to honor the Sherpas who perished. Lakpa knew most of them so he told us stories about their lives and how desperate they were to earn money for their families. He had been instrumental in lobbying the government and climbing companies to provide compensation to the families of the deceased. Lakpa was very emotional as he talked to us, unable to control his grief and sadness. It was impossible to look at this proud, courageous man without losing control ourselves and we all dissolved in tears.

I left immediately after the ceremony and returned to my tent because I couldn't hold all the grief I was feeling. I couldn't stop crying and I wasn't sure why exactly. I'm on this mountain to help save Nepali people, but I realized, all at once, that in doing so I was also putting other Nepali lives in jeopardy. I knew that being selected as an Everest Sherpa, porter, or "icefall doctor" was a great privilege that would earn them 10 times what they could make on just a trekking trip. I understood that there were hundreds, if not thousands, of others who would take these jobs if they could get them, as if they hit the jackpot. This is a country where the average annual income is just a few hundred dollars and yet a climbing Sherpa on Everest can earn as much as $5,000 during a season. Nevertheless, I felt sad that people would have to risk their lives every day to escort people like me to the top of the mountain.

Practice and Training

I was quite aware that climbing Everest was not like anything I'd ever attempted before. Sure, I'd been at high altitude on Cho Oyu that was almost comparable, but the additional few thousand feet in the "death zone" made this climb infinitely more difficult. In addition, there was a fair bit of technical climbing that would be required, not just to get through the Icefall but also on the Hillary Step right before the summit. Then there were all the crowds that were vying to get to the summit, dozens of different teams from various countries that would slow us down while we waited for struggling climbers to negotiate certain parts where we could only pass through one at a time. Sometimes people have to wait in line for hours to get through certain sections. That's when people freeze to death, or their window of opportunity closes.

We were scheduled to spend the next week practicing and training, testing our endurance and skills so the guides could assess our readiness. They took us out on ice walls to practice crampon and ax techniques. We practiced rappelling off of cliffs, crossing ladders in our heavy boots with all our equipment, and self-arrest techniques, if one of us slipped off a glacier or fell into a crevasse, very real possibilities. The one thing we didn't prepare much for were avalanches because, frankly, in much of the terrain there's not much you can do except pray.

Even though it felt like that in some ways I was living in a vibrant city with all the noise, parties going on, music blaring, and conversations I could hear through the walls of my tent, I was often reminded that we were all sitting in a very precarious, isolated, wild part of Nature. The howling winds were so strong during a few of the nights, pummeling the tent, there was no way to get any sleep. I kept thinking all night long what I'd do if the wind just lifted me up and dropped me in a crevasse.

Even with the trouble sleeping and chronic headache, I still had to remain focused on our grueling training regimen. We would go into the Icefall most days and practice safety techniques and crossing ladders as fast as possible. This is one of the most dangerous places in the world, where

Climbing practice in the Khumbu Icefall

fissures in the ice open with no warning, toppling ice towers as tall as build-ings that guard the entrances to routes up and over the obstacles. More people die here than anywhere else on the mountain and it's almost always a random, unavoidable set of circumstances. So whenever I was in this magi-cal, beautiful, dangerous place, it felt like I was holding my breath, waiting for something really bad to happen. While navigating ourselves through, around, and over the ice barriers, I was constantly thinking about how this mountain could swallow me up in an instant: one minute I'd be striding along, the next moment the ice would split open and I'd fall through.

The worst part of our exercises involved crossing the ladders suspended over open crevasses. Sometimes, two ladders are lashed together because the opening is too wide; at other times, the ladders are attached at a slight angle, or tipped upward to crawl over a wall. Just imagine how terrifying it might be to walk across a ladder suspended over an endless, gaping hole in the ground, one that is so deep that even if you had the courage to look straight down, you wouldn't see the bottom. Now picture doing this while wearing huge, unwieldy, heavy boots with the soles lashed to a dozen sharp spikes that clank awkwardly with every step. Add to this challenge that you are also wearing a heavy backpack, throwing your center of gravity off balance. Oh yes, it could also be wickedly icey on the ladder in a blizzard and the wind could be blowing 50 miles an hour.

When returning from one of the practice sessions, I ran into Azim, the Iranian climber who had summited all the highest mountains on Earth without oxygen. He was hard to miss in a bright yellow, puffy jacket. "I was watching you today," he said as he approached.

"You were?"

"Yes, I notice you walk so fast on the mountain. You must slow down and save your energy. Take lazy steps."

I just nodded dumbly, unsure how to respond. This guy was a climbing superstar, a god, and he was giving me advice and telling me he thinks I have potential. He invited me to come by his tent later for Iranian tea and Persian snacks, a real treat. While we snacked on pistachios, crackers, and sipped our tea, Azim gave me advice about some things I might do to better control the dryness of my throat, explaining that cough drops would help.

Later that day, it was really warm out for a change and I was walking around in just a tee shirt, when Azim scolded me once again that I was wasting energy by letting my own heat escape. He also warned me that the intensity of the sun reflected off the snow would burn me to a crisp if I wasn't careful. Suitably chastised, I immediately covered up. I felt so grateful that I had a climbing angel, an Iranian brother, who was looking out for me.

Camp One

It was finally time for us to start relocating ourselves up to Camp One, which made me nervous because that meant we'd have to get all the way through the Icefall, and then back again after some acclimatizing time. On our first attempt, our plan was just to make it as far as we could, then turn back, just so we'd become more familiar with the terrain and more comfortable balancing ourselves when we crossed the ladders. This was so much harder than I thought it would be when I practiced at home. For one thing, sometimes I could feel the glacier shifting. Secondly, the ladders were often wobbly and felt unstable. And thirdly, the rungs on the ladders weren't always a uniform distance from one another so it meant that each step with crampons had to be carefully planned—and this required looking down frequently, which gave me vertigo peering into the abyss.

Everyone on our team was encouraging, with Aussie Jon most of all. He was just always cheerful about everything, as if he didn't have a care in the world, and this felt contagious and reassuring. His tent was a little bigger than the rest of ours so he called it "the mansion" and would frequently invite us over to play games or hang out.

Just before we were about to leave I confessed to Aussie Jon that I was scared and apprehensive about our trip so far into the Icefall. There was something disconcerting about the idea that at any minute the Earth could open up and eat me, or else a huge building of solid ice could fall on top of me. "You can do this," he reassured me. "We'll take care of one another. The odds of falling into a crevasse are pretty remote—and even if that happens, we'll just pull you out." Then he grinned and in that typical Australian way, lightly punched me in the arm and said, "No worries, mate."

I went back to my tent and felt I was finally ready to read the letter in the envelope that my friend, Pari gave me at the airport with instructions to read when I was having some doubts and fears. Truthfully, I was terrified going through the Icefall. Yes, it was gorgeous. Some of the time it was really fun climbing up ice towers and traversing the jigsaw puzzle pieces of ice that sometimes blocked our way. But there was also something formidable and menacing about the place. With every step I wondered if I was walking on top of someone else's buried body.

In the letter, Pari reminded me that I chose to be vulnerable and take a risk in beginning this whole enterprise. She told me that I wasn't doing this alone, although sometimes it felt that way. That she was with me. That all my friends and family were with me. I burst into tears as I tucked the letter back into my duffel and started organizing my equipment for the next day's departure. It would be April 25 and so far I'd been in Nepal for a month.

We woke up really early the next morning to have breakfast because it was going to be a long, tiring day. My backpack was loaded with all the stuff I'd need for a few days before we returned, and I felt wobbly just trying to remain upright until I could find my stride.

In some ways, it was almost a relief that the visibility wasn't that great with blowing snow as it helped me to keep my focus only on looking at the small space right in front of my next, careful step. We made excellent progress, keeping up a slow, steady pace until we reached a towering ice wall just ahead. Camp One was located on top of the ridge. Now we just had to negotiate five vertical ladders that were connected to one another and attached to the wall rather than use our ice axes and crampons to climb the ice. The ladders made this stage so much easier.

We took one last rest perched on top of a serac, an ice tower with a flat top that we'd had to climb over. We were all too tired to talk so we just sat there, numb, trying to drink some water and eat a snack. We would be arriving at Camp One in less than an hour.

Damian went first on the ladders, then Mack, then I would follow next. When I heard Mack yell, "Clear," it meant he was off the rope and ladder so it was my turn. I stopped for a moment to look around and grinned at my teammates waiting at the bottom. For the first time in a while I felt really strong, really good. We were at 20,000 feet and I realized I no longer had any altitude symptoms. I don't know if it was my excitement, my new-found strength, or some premonition, but I scurried up those ladders just as fast as I could climb—until just before I reached the top

I remembered Azim's advice to slow down. "Take lazy steps, just lazy steps," I could hear him whispering in my ear.

I was almost at the top, my arms and legs feeling rubbery, my breathing labored, when all of a sudden I could feel the ladder start to vibrate, then shake and begin to pull loose from the wall. I held on as tightly as I could, but it felt like the whole world was ending.

What's that sound?

CHAPTER 15

—— ❧ ——

Sara and Jeffrey: Aftermath

July, 2016

WE BOTH CONFESS that our visits to Nepal these past few years have been among the most fulfilling, satisfying, and joyful experiences of our lives—and also the most challenging and traumatic. Each of us struggles with our own ghosts and nightmares. Friends and acquaintances we know have been seriously injured; others have died. Many are still without homes and several have lost all hope and disappeared.

This has also been a period of difficult transitions for us. Jeffrey has since retired from the foundation and is struggling to let go of the charity he built from scratch, beginning with one girl he saved so long ago. In order for any organization to survive, much less flourish, the original founder has to get out of the way and allow new leadership team members to impose their own vision on where they wish things to go. But after so much devotion, energy, commitment, time, money, and deep love for the children and volunteers, it's really, really hard to walk away.

Sara, on the other hand, is now taking on more and more responsibilities for raising funds, conducting media interviews, mentoring the children, and joining the Board of Directors after being invited to do so by the new president. Although she has a clear vision of what she wants to do to lend assistance to the children and the role she wants to play in their lives, so many other aspects of her life remain in flux. She wonders how the girls can follow her footsteps when she is now uncertain about where her life is heading.

It is commonly reported by teachers, counselors, therapists, and other professionals, that often we are changed as much by our helping efforts as those we assisted. We are haunted and so moved by their stories. We learn so much about others' lives, and in so doing, we are offered a window to explore more deeply what gives our own lives the most meaning and satisfaction. For Sara, that means she has discovered new aspects of herself, as well as other parts that have long been obsolete. She is no longer working as an engineer and computer professor but has decided to devote her life to advocacy and leadership, enrolling in a doctoral program to better prepare herself for the next stages. Sara and Matt are beginning to talk about starting a family soon, but first they have some traveling to get out of their systems—and perhaps a few more mountains to climb.

Painful Lessons

Everest is probably not in Sara's future, although she still feels a restless yearning to take care of that unfinished business. Although this year was a banner season for summiting the world's highest peak, with hundreds of people managing to get to the top, there have also been senseless, random deaths with several climbers who had reached the summit and then just keeled over dead from acute altitude sickness on the way down. Their bodies just suddenly shut down for no other apparent reason.

That gives Sara pause about the extent to which she is still willing to risk her life just to climb a mountain. This lesson hit her particularly hard on the exact day of the anniversary of the first earthquake and avalanche. It had already been a difficult time for Sara, crying inconsolably as she continued to have flashbacks to that awful day, and the weeks that followed, with so many people dead and homeless, and so many horrible memories that still plagued her. But then news came to magnify the suffering and bring home the lessons learned.

Aussie Jon had been climbing Shishapangma, the last 8,000 meter Himalayan peak to be climbed as a result of its isolated location in the Chinese-controlled region of Tibet. His wife and son had spoken to him via satellite phone the day before and he was feeling strong, fit, and ecstatic about the progress thus far. They had just returned from an acclimatizing hike to 20,000 feet and things had gone extraordinarily well. Jon was optimistic about the next day's plan as well and felt somewhat wistful because it was exactly one year since they'd been trapped on Everest.

Jon was roped together with another climber and a guide, on their way to Camp One, when they stopped mid-day for a rest. Suddenly, without any warning, the ground underneath them opened up into a deep, narrow crevasse, swallowing the three of them. It was a 100-foot fall into a narrow cave, knocking the climbers unconscious. There was a rescue attempt by another team that had been following, but they were only able to reach the guide who was the last to fall in. Jon and his companion were trapped in the narrow, inaccessible space with no visible movements. The rescuers were unable to retrieve the bodies.

Sara had just spoken to Jon a few weeks earlier when he called to get some advice about climbing in Tibet. He wanted to know details about how much oxygen he would need, what equipment was useful. They had a chance to reconnect and reminisce about the time they spent together and what an amazing team they had on Everest, certain they would have summited if things had turned out differently. Sara was so excited for Jon's latest adventure and just knew he would do well on Shishapangma because he was the strongest of all of them.

Notification of Jon's death was just one more burden for Sara to carry on an already miserable day. There had been postings all over social media, bringing attention to the anniversary of the earthquakes and how so little had changed since then. All Sara could think about was Jon's wife and children who no longer had a father. "I just couldn't hold myself together any longer. We were in a restaurant when I made another scene by sobbing out loud. Of course everyone was freaked out and tried to reassure me that I'd be okay, but it just didn't feel that way."

Jon's random death only reinforced in Sara's mind that no matter how hard you prepare and train for a challenge, there is still only so much you

*My friend and former climbing partner on Everest,
"Aussie Jon," was tragically killed falling into a Himalayan
crevasse that opened underneath him. Ironically, this
occurred on the one year anniversary of our survival
form the earthquake and avalanche on Everest.*

can do to maintain an illusion of control over your own welfare and fate. Sara had already survived so many close calls that she wondered if her own luck was running out. Nevertheless, there were so many children depending on her that she has to find a way to keep the momentum going, without having to recklessly put her own life in jeopardy.

Members of the Everest team started to reach out to one another for support. Kate, Sara's tent mate, called several times, as did several of the guides. They traded favorite photos of Jon's, updates from the family, and like all mountaineers, wanted details of what happened and why, as if such knowledge would ward off future dangers. But there's not much you can do to protect yourself against the ground opening up beneath you without warning.

After his own close calls during the earthquakes, and his own mountaineering experiences, Jeffrey has also vowed to slow down, mostly as a function of advancing age. During the last trip to Nepal, Jeffrey had to be hospitalized twice because of serious health problems that resulted from bacterial food poisoning. He lost so much weight that he had to discard his previous wardrobe because his body had been reshaped from the illnesses. He now has had to come to terms with the reality that there are some things he just can't do anymore.

The Anniversary

April 25 will always be a date cemented in our memories, the anniversary of the earthquakes. In some ways, nothing much has changed in Nepal. The government is still as corrupt and incompetent as ever. Much of the money donated by foreign governments or aid agencies has either disappeared, been squandered, or sits idle and wasted. There are still fuel shortages, housing shortages, and very little rebuilding that has taken place.

We have all worked furiously during the last year to do our part to help with the recovery. All of our volunteers, staff, and team members have been actively involved in raising as much money as we can, enough so that we have been able to provide additional scholarships to needy girls, supply equipment and resources to schools that were damaged, as well as fund our earthquake relief efforts. A number of corporate entities like PayPal, Microsoft, Oracle, and eBay have jumped on board and provided resources for our children. As word has spread that we are one of the few charities operating under the radar, with minimal overhead and expenses, we have been able to triple our operating budget. That's the good news.

The bad news, of course, is that many of our girls are still homeless and without basic necessities. Most of the schools our children attend have been damaged significantly and limit even further certain educational opportunities. With continuous strikes, political squabbling, and heated conflicts among the dozen different political parties, it has been impossible for the government to reach consensus and move forward in a productive way.

Sara speaking to a group of elementary school children about her adventures as a mountain climber and her efforts to support girls in Nepal

We couldn't let these things discourage our efforts. One of the things our Nepali girls have taught us over the years is that it is best to just ignore what the government officials are doing—or not doing—to ignore the strikes and shortages and disappointments, and just persevere. So that's what we've been trying to do.

Everywhere she would go, and at every fundraiser where she would speak, people would ask Sara if she was going to try to summit Everest again.

Sara would pause for a moment and consider the question and how best to answer it. "I have a feeling," she would reply, "that I already reached the top of Everest. Perhaps not the mountain itself, but my own Everest." All along, Sara's main goal was to raise money to support the girls; the mountains were just a way, admittedly an exciting, fun, painful way, to accomplish this task

"If I go back anytime, it would be for raising funds and awareness again for women and girls around the world. I just don't want to climb Everest by myself. I would like to take a group of girls and women who are trying to get there, or improve themselves, or learn something in the process. I want to train somebody else to go with me rather than just myself going up there. I thought it would be amazing if I could gather a group of women from all over the world, one from Iran, one from Nepal, one from the United States, one from Africa, or anywhere else in the world, and we all train together, and we climb together. And on top of the mountain we stand together representing all the women in the world. That would be something to motivate me to climb such a mountain again."

Life Goes On

Most of our girls have tried to patch their lives back together. Some of them are now living with relatives, others have been placed in temporary housing or we have arranged to rent rooms for them. We first began this effort so many years ago when the cost to keep a girl in school was less than $50 per year—and that included school fees, books, uniforms, and supplies. Now that so many of our girls are older and attending higher education, the cost per girl now exceeds several thousand dollars each year for technical, medical, or nursing studies. We feel even more pressure to keep the momentum going with so many children whose very lives depend on our efforts to help support them.

Our own lives have changed as well during this time. Sara's family has been somewhat fractured these past years, which is what led her to create some distance and separation from them. But the combination of a crisis with her brother, as well as her family's incessant worry about Sara's safety and welfare, has brought everyone much closer together. That has been one of the gifts that has resulted from all the suffering and sacrifices. Sara now feels closer to her mother, and especially her father, than ever before. They talk more regularly and Sara has been much more open with them about her life, her dreams, and her future plans. Yes, she still gets a lot of pressure to settle down and make babies, and that will happen soon enough, but for now she and Matt plan to travel and figure out where they will live next. Between her fundraising efforts, new doctoral studies, and teaching responsibilities, she is plenty busy, but not so much that it interferes with her next adventure.

Jeffrey and Sara both have faced some of their greatest fears during the events that unfolded in this story. Sara has faced so many challenges, including the fear of death of course, but also fear of the cold, of the dark, of asking for money, of being alone, of public speaking, and of suffering.

"I have never lived my life more fully," Sara believes, "than I have during this last year. I have never felt more alive, more engaged, more passionate and excited about what I'm doing. And I can readily see how contagious this has been for others, including my family, friends, and our girls in Nepal. I hear so much envy and jealousy from others: How can you do these things? How can you afford to do these things? How do you find the time? How do you put up with all the aggravation and difficulties? When people hear some of my stories of where I've been and what I've done, they just roll their eyes and say, 'Better you than me.' But that's not quite true. All my life I have been waiting and waiting for the perfect time to do perfect things that I always wanted to do, but fear and excuses always stood in my way. I think there is no perfect time to start any new endeavor; there are always reasons to postpone. When I started mountain climbing, it was in the middle of winter with no team or crew at the beginning, with no training, no gear, no mentor, and no clear reason to do this in the first place except an impulsive gesture. But little by little, the universe gave me all that I needed, and ever wanted, and even more. The earthquakes were absolutely tragic and devastating, but this is what we got from the universe, and I accept that. Mother Goddess Sagarmāthā, also known as Mt. Everest, didn't want me up there, and I accept it fully with all my heart. It's time for me to come back down to Earth."

Three of our older scholarship girls who are now attending higher education to pursue careers in finance, banking, and computer science. They are the first girls in their village to attend college or university.

For Jeffrey, his learning curve at this latter stage of life, is about moving on to the next thing. For so long, he has been the one in control, the one with the vision and energy to make things happen, whether in the classroom, writing several new books each year, or trying to advocate on behalf of girls in Nepal. If our work continues, however, this will be the result of the collective efforts of so many of our volunteers, team members, and donors who can take things to the next level. The hardest lesson for a leader is knowing when it's time to let go, move on, and allow others to take a turn.

Facing challenges, taking risks, tackling the things that frighten us the most, are precisely the things that have most empowered us, as well as inspiring our girls to follow in our footsteps. These girls are attempting something that is absolutely unprecedented, to become the first ones in their villages to attain an education and pursue a professional career. They will become engineers, psychologists, mountaineers, or professors like us. They will demonstrate to their families and communities that they are indeed among their country's greatest resources who will someday transform their nation. That is our hope and dream.

Made in the USA
Charleston, SC
23 July 2016